SCHOLAR, PRIEST, AND PASTOR

Ministry Priorities Among Clergy Today

...a study of stress & satisfaction in the work place...

Methodist + Lutheran + Catholic + Episcopal

John H. Morgan

GTF Books

SCHOLAR, PRIEST, AND PASTOR

Ministry Priorities Among Clergy Today
...a study of stress & satisfaction in the work place...

by John H. Morgan

Library of Congress Catalog Card Number

97-61551

International Standard Book Number

1-55605-278-2 (Paperback)

Published by GTF Books (USA)

Distributed by Wyndham Hall Press (USA)

To Vincent,
Scholar and Priest,
Pastor and Friend.

...books by John H. Morgan...

Studies in Ecclesiastical Sociology

> *The Diaconate Today: A Study of Clergy Attitudes*
> *Who Becomes Bishop?: A Study of Episcopal Priests*
> *Women Priests: A Study of an Emerging Ministry*
> *Wives of Priests: A Study of Episcopal Clergy Spouses (with Linda B. Morgan)*
> *Scholar, Priest, and Pastor: Ministry Priorities Among Clergy Today*

Theology and the Social Sciences

> *In Search of Meaning: From Freud to Teilhard de Chardin*
> *The Anglican Mind: A Theological Compendium (17th Century English Thought)*
> *Catholic Spirituality: A Guide for Protestants*
> *Understanding Religion and Culture: Essays in Honor of Clifford Geertz*
> *Sociological Thought from Comte to Sorokin (with M. F. Abraham)*
> *From Freud to Frankl: Our Modern Search for Personal Meaning*
> *The United Inheritance: The Shaker Adventure in Communal Life*
> *Interfacing Geertz and Tillich: A Convergence of Meaning*

Research Tools and Methodologies

> *Library Research in Sociology*
> *Library Research in Psychology*
> *Sociopharmacology: A Research Bibliography*
> *Genetics and Behavior: A Research Bibliography*
> *Sociobiology: A Research Bibliography*

Poetry Anthologies and Celebrations

> *Celebrating T. S. Eliot: Contemporary Poetry on the Eliot Centennial*
> *Newman of Oxford: A Centennial Celebration in Poetry*
> *Frost in Spring: An Anthology in Memoriam to Robert Frost*

ACKNOWLEDGMENTS

With better than fifty years' involvement in the life of the church, I find myself overwhelmed with the responsibility of identifying those individuals who have had a part, one way or the other, in the creation of this book. If one were to say, as in the old spiritual "...all God's children, then and now...," that would just about do it. However, naming names and giving thanks is part of the act of gratitude and so must it be here. To name names is possible; to place them in order of importance is not.

Needless to say, I must thank my dear father who, during his life, taught me by example to love the church and seek always to serve Her as best I could. My mother has quietly gone about encouraging me to do just that; indeed, she even helped stuff the envelopes and do the mailing for this survey. To both father and mother, I am eternally grateful.

Robley E. Whitson was the first Catholic priest I ever knew. I spent four years in seminary studying at his feet and I have yet to elevate myself from that posture of respect and reverence for who he is and what he has done for me in my professional and spiritual growth. He is both the consummate teacher and colleague, and my life will forever be altered for having encountered him early in my journey into the life of Christ.

To the Rev'd. Canon Vincent Strudwick of Kellogg College/Oxford, I owe much. He brought me into involvement in the life of Oxford in ways I could have only dreamed of before knowing him. He put me on the Board of Studies of the University of Oxford's Summer Program in Theology, and in that capacity, I have come to know the grandeur of the University and the vitality of its intellectual life. And to Dr. John Macquarrie for so readily accepting me and his continued support and encouragement at Oxford, I will always be appreciative. Canon John Fenton and Dr. Tom and Barbara Tinsley, all of Oxford, have enriched my life there and my work here. To Sister Raymunda Jordan, OP, thanks unlimited for her willingness to share her ministry at every stage with me as I struggle in admiration to understand the scope and depth of her service to the church. To Father James Puglisi, SA, of the Centro Pro Unione in Rome, who provided me a model of priestly ii

dedication to an unrelenting search for a fuller and more nurturing vision of the church, I will forever be admiringly grateful. And, not least, to Father Tom Ryan, who is the embodiment of all that is good and hopeful about the priesthood as lived out in the life of a dedicated Irish priest from County Clare, thanks for everything.

Institutions are legion in my life and though there are always real people behind the doors and walls and windows of such places, I nevertheless wish never to fail to mention the ones which have blessed my life with their favors, including Oxford, Harvard, Yale, Princeton, the University of Notre Dame, and the University of Chicago. At each institution and at a crucial moment in my life, I found hope and encouragement and promise of things to come.

To the Poor Handmaids of Jesus Christ and their lovely home, Convent Ancilla Domini in Indiana, where I make my theological dwelling and enjoy the operational management of the Graduate Theological Foundation, I am filled with gratitude for their hospitality.

To Valerie Relos, Registrar of the Foundation and chief administrator of my comings and goings on its behalf, for all of the encouragement I will always be thankful.

Finally, to my family, Linda, Kendra, Bethany, Kyna, and Milton, from whom I daily draw love and hope and promise, thank you all. And to my old dog, Sable, who missed her walks about the farm because she knew I was busy but never really understood exactly what it was that seemed to her companion more important than a walk in the fields anyway, thanks old girl.

Ancilla Domini/Donaldson
Spring, 1998

PREFACE

"Gladly would he learn, and gladly teach." So says The Canterbury Tales as they speak of the Oxford don. And so with the author of this study. Twenty-five years in higher education and all of my life in the midst of the church and surrounded by Her clergy, this is my experience and this is my passion. This book is only one of many written in the tradition of "ecclesiastical sociology," that is, sociological analysis of matters related to the life of the church by one involved in that faith and practice. It is sociology from inside the community of faith not unlike the Venerable Bede's *Ecclesiastical History*. History he wrote, but history from within the church.

The following study is based on standard sociological methods and theories but applied to a study of the clergy from one who is a follower of Christ and a lover of His church. If this is a weakness, let the accuser step forward and identify other criteria which are more acceptable. If I loved the church less, could I understand Her clergy better? Who is to say? I can only report who I am and what I have attempted to do in this and many other similar studies, namely, identify problems and issues based on empirical data gathered from the real sources of factual information and then attempt to convey my findings and offer suggestions for further understanding to those who might benefit from such information. If I fail in my attempt, the effort has nevertheless been an exercise of love and passion and the intentions were good even if the results fall short. If, on the other hand, anything suggested herein proves of benefit to anyone in ministry or in the leadership of the church, then all of the effort was well worth it.

The following study is divided into four chapters of data analysis, three bibliographical resources, and three appendices. The five chapters cover the full scope of the data gathered and analyzed in this major investigation of clergy perceptions of their roles and their perceptions of what they believe their communities to expect of them. In other words, it is a study in ministry priorities as reflected in stress and satisfaction variables in the work place.

Chapter one introduces and explains the background to the purpose of this study with particular attention given to identifying strengths and weaknesses in each of the four traditions studied here, viz., Methodist, Lutheran, Catholic, and Episcopalian (Anglican). Chapter Two constitutes a careful recitation of the research methodology employed in this data-based study, building upon the sociological notion of "domain assumptions" and the use of the questionnaire (the research instrument) in the gathering of clergy "perceptions" of themselves and their communities. Chapter Three explores what we have chosen to label "indigenous analysis," which is to say a careful investigation of fifteen information categories within each tradition. We avoided any "comparison" of data here across tradition lines in an attempt to be fully focused and fair in our analysis of each tradition. In Chapter Four, we employed intentionally the "comparative" perspective in an attempt to tease out further insights into the data gathered from the four traditions.

Following the study itself, there are three resource bibliographies for the interested student and scholar. The first gives the data-based reference for all nationally authorized statistics on the four denominations used herein. Second, there is a listing of a few of the major works in the field valued by this author as crucial to the study. Finally, there is a general resource bibliography for those interested in doing further reading and research in ministry as a profession.

Finally, there are three appendices included in this book. Each is designed to demonstrate either the theoretical infrastructure of ecclesiastical sociology as a behavioral science or to demonstrate a different kind of application of the theory and method to a non-data-based topic. The essay on phenomenological sociology is an attempt to explore the theoretical infrastructures for those interested in the philosophical background and implications of this approach to data analysis. The essay on pastoral ecstasy attempts to demonstrate the application of social analysis to studies of the self and its implications for ministry. And lastly, there is an exploration into the concept of hermeneutics as an interpretive methodology.

It is hoped that the book stands on its own without benefit of bibliographies and appendices. Yet, it is also hoped that the added features of bibliographies and appendices will be valued by the reader as meriting the effort.

TABLE OF CONTENTS

CHAPTER ONE

PURPOSE OF THIS STUDY
"...avoiding conflict and seeking satisfaction..."

"Since the Second Vatican Council, everything has changed." This was a comment I recently overhead at a gathering of clergy at the University of Oxford where a Catholic Cardinal had just given an address. It sounded so simplistic, even naive, in its singularity of focus. What could "everything" mean in this context? Had there not been change before Vatican II? Would it not be a bit more telling to say "some things are changing" rather than "everything has changed"? I pondered the statement and considered the context and framework -- the context was an address by one of England's most noted churchmen in one of the world's most respected centers of learning within the framework of a discussion of the ministry in the coming 21st century.

My interest initially was not so much that set by the gathering in Oxford, i.e., looking squint-eyed into the 21st century at the church and Her ministry, but rather a deeply felt need to explore the presently existing pressures and shifting expectations experienced by the clergy here and now. From the 19th century to the 21st century is a màjor leap in consciousness about ministry and socio-cultural and professional expectations and demands. The 19th century clergy had what by all accounts was a rather more or less clear-eyed understanding of what was demanded by the ministry and what was needed to prepare for those demands. The 21st century is fuzzy and unclear to us just now. The present situation of clergy in the parish, however, is rather immediate and full-faced in its character and presentation. The pressures are real and they are now. The shifts in expectations from within the parish and among the clergy are occurring as we speak, somewhat like observing molecular growth under a microscope in a research lab. Following the church papers, daily, weekly, and monthly, is enough to identify the shifting and transforming and evolving and devolving of expectations, demands, hopes, fears, and quandries occurring within the ministry.

The ministry as a profession is in warp-time transformation inter- and intra-denominationally. There is no religious community which is not aware of this reality. Whether one talks with the bishops of the Old Mennonite Order of Believers or the bishops of the Roman Catholic Church, awareness of change is everywhere. "Any change affects everything," to quote a mathematical truism. Denominational executives, seminary deans, bishops, superintendents, parish councils, and directors of religious education all face the exponential shifts and transformations being brought on by the postconciliar encounter with world liberation, gender consciousness-raising, third-world economic growth, multi-culturalism, and the like. The composition of seminaries today, whether Protestant or Catholic, is merely a laboratory display of a universal phenomenon. Not just the student body -- gender, race, ethnicity, nationality, etc. -- but equally the faculty and the curriculum and the administrative decisions about institutional management and program design all are indicative of this awareness of change. To say "everything has changed" is quite decidedly not a profound statement, but, without doubt, it is a true one. What is meant by this statement as it relates to ministry in the church today is the impetus for this study and has led to the writing of this book.

"Don't worry, be happy" the popular Caribbean tune chants to a troubled and stress-ridden world and we all think, "Why not?" Singing and holding hands, we have found out in the civil rights movement of the 60s, is not quite enough if things are going to change for the better. Avoiding conflict and seeking satisfaction is without doubt a reasonable mode of operation but how to actually do it is not quite as simple as merely saying it.

From the beginning of my interest in doing this study and writing the book, I knew the church was not in need of yet another speculative treatise on the why's and why not's, the ways and means, the how-to's and how-not-to's of problem-solving in the profession of ministry. Armchair ecclesiastical cant we have enough of already, and the well-intentioned theologian or historian or religious philosopher who expounds yet another theory or hypothesis or who postulates another scenario of solutions and suggestions is making little difference in the absence of "factual" identification of those factors which bring on stress or usher in satisfaction within the parish and within the life of the clergy. If we could only get our hands on actual information rather than well-intentioned spin-doctoring, then we would at least have an empirical basis to launch a discussion and establish an agenda for the future. This, needless

SCHOLAR, PRIEST, AND PASTOR   3

to say, constitutes my framework of reference. Give me hard facts every time before I am asked to identify a problem and propose an agenda for problem-solving.

What, I ask myself, is wrong with finding out what clergy are actually experiencing? And why not have *them* indicate what *they* perceive to be the nature of the real world in which they minister? To do this, I determined to create a research instrument which would solicit real information about real activities and real perceptions of the social landscape *as seen by the clergy*. I wanted real information, real facts, real "data," if you will. Furthermore, I wanted to concentrate upon four mainline denominations in the United States, two large ones and two smaller ones with massive memberships and thousands of parishes and clergy all over the country. I chose the United Methodist Church (called throughout merely "Methodists"), the Evangelical Lutheran Church of America (called throughout merely "Lutherans" with full cognizance of the many and significant differences among the various bodies of Lutherans), the Roman Catholic Church (called "Catholics") and the Episcopal Church U.S.A. (referred to variously as "Episcopal" and "Anglican").

The numbers are impressive and any researcher would delight at the prospects of dipping a research instrument into these large bodies of laity and clergy. I wanted to conduct what I like to think of as a data-base biopsy whereby a laboratory analysis of collected samples renders a reasonable picture of the entire body. The sizes of these four denominations commended themselves to this type of study. The Methodists have over 36,000 congregations and eight and a half million members with half of their 38,000 clergy serving in parish ministry. The Lutherans have nearly eleven thousand congregations and five million members served by 17,000 clergy, half of whom work in the parish setting. The Catholics have nearly 20,000 congregations and over sixty million members served by almost 50,000 clergy. The Episcopal church U.S.A. has nearly 7,500 parishes with 1.5 million confirmed members and 15,000 clergy with better than half of them in parish ministry. (source: *Yearbook of American and Canadian Churches 1997*, edited by Kenneth B. Bedell, published by Abingdon of Nashville and sponsored by the National Council of Churches of Christ).

Editorial Note: At the risk of appearing insensitive to gender-neutral language issues and with the support of my publisher, I have chosen to use masculine references as "gender-generic" rather than the cumbersome he/she, him/her, etc. The author is fully aware of the reality of women clergy, indeed, I have written more than one book on the subject. But, at the end of the day, the book reads more smoothly written the old-fashioned way.

CHAPTER TWO

METHODOLOGY
"...asking questions and getting answers..."

It is characteristic of my shopping habits to enter a store and spend useless time wandering up and down the aisles in search of an item with the end result being that I am finally forced to ask a helpful clerk who easily and readily directs me to the desired item. Every time I enter a store I make a personal commitment to ask for help before beginning the search. I seldom remember the commitment, and, thus, am doomed to repeat the same old self-defeating agenda over and over again. I often feel this way when questions regarding the ministry arise. The church seems to be replete with individuals quite willing to endlessly wander the aisles in search of an answer without ever pausing to consider whether it would be a more effective technique to actually direct the question to the individual concerned. If we want to know how much time a pastor spends preparing a sermon, why not ask? If we are curious about the attitude clergy have regarding their ministry in the community, why not ask?

PERCEIVED REALITY ... "The World as I See It"

Another dimension, indeed, the most telling and fascinating dimension to this business of asking questions and getting answers, has to do with "perception of reality." That is to say, if we are interested in how a priest conducts himself in light of what he thinks the parish expects of him, then by asking him to answer questions regarding this conduct and his attendant view of the parish, we are not so much hoping to find out "the real truth" about the parish's expectation as we are to find out the real truth "as the priest sees it." In sociology, we call this the *social construction of reality*, which really simply means we are concerned with how the priest "perceives" the parish expectation and then its resultant response in conditioned behavior. One might argue that we could never really find out the actual truth in this situation and even if we did that would be of precious little use in trying to understand the priest's

6 John H. Morgan

behavior since he is responding not to what we have established as "the real truth" but what he perceives to be the real truth.

Therefore, what has been done in the research instrument is to ask the clergy to respond both to their feelings or attitudes about a particular concern and then also to indicate what they think to be the attitude of the parish about the same concern. Whether the clergy accurately perceive the parish's mind is impossible to tell, but what is important to note is that in light of how the clergy "perceive" the parish, in that same light they choose to respond. Behavior is never in response to the metaphysical truth but is in response to the truth as perceived by the observer. In sociology we call this "perceived reality," and that constitutes the basis for the discussion which follows here.

If the priest "thinks" the congregation resents the amount of time he spends working on his sermon, then that perception is vitally important in understanding his response to what he thinks to be true much more than what might "really" be true if we were "all knowing." Truth in this context is strictly and solely subjective truth, truth as seen by the priest, and not objective abstract truth known only to God. In dealing with human truth rather than Divine Truth, we are encountering the world as constructed by those who see it and those who respond to that which they see in it.

DOMAIN ASSUMPTIONS ... Operative Presuppositions and Functional Stereotypes

An initial set of presuppositions, or undefended stereotypes, was identified early in the development of this study. These "domain assumptions," as sociologists like to call them, were "in the air," presumed to be true and accurate without any intention or desire to test whether they were or not. They constitute a beginning place, if you will, and the success or failure of the database study does not live or die with their accuracy. They merely constitute a starting place for enquiry. We began with three domain assumptions and with three sets of stereotypical concepts regarding ministry.

The three domain assumptions were that of the four traditions being investigated here, viz., Methodist, Lutheran, Catholic, Episcopal, with each one more or less embodying a particular view of the clergy. The particular view of the clergy constituted three sets of stereotypes, viz., scholar, priest, pastor. On the basis of historical development within each tradition, it was assumed that the Methodist clergy would be more likely to identify themselves as "pastors," the Lutherans as "scholars," the Catholics as "priests," and the Episcopal clergy as equivocally "pastor" and "priest," depending on the churchmanship of the parish. Thus, the beginning of the book and its title. This starting point allowed us to construct the research instrument, i.e., the questionnaire, and thereby constituted the launching pad for the gathering and analyzing of the data.

The domain assumptions are not so far fetched as one might presume at the outset. If one thinks of the Catholic priesthood and the origin and history of the term and its attendant characteristics from the earliest Apostolic days down to the present, the fact that Catholic clergy think of themselves as primarily "priests" rather than pastors or scholars begins to take on historical reality. Likewise, if one takes full cognizance of the history of the Lutheran tradition and the birth of the Reformation movement, with, on the one hand, its anti-clericalism, and on the other, its "sola Scriptura" emphasis as well as its emphasis upon scholarship, one seems not to have gone far astray in suggesting that the Lutheran church's clergy might rightfully think of themselves in the tradition of "scholars" rather than priests or pastors. Furthermore, when thinking of Methodists, one must remember the history of the Wesley brothers, their Anglican origins and priestly roles in the church of England and all that resulted from their disenfranchisement from the Established church. With their primary emphasis upon the nurture of souls, it seems only right and proper that the term "pastor" be applied generously to the Methodist clergy. Here again, the Episcopal clergy in America constitute something of a quandry to be settled later. Thus, the domain assumptions were born and carried forth in this study. At the end of the study, we will revisit these domain assumptions and assess their viability and utility.

In constructing the survey, we drew heavily upon our stereotypical description of the three categories of clergy functions, i.e., scholar, priest, pastor. We designed the questionnaire such that the questions would search out tell-tale signs of scholarly, priestly, or pastoral self-understanding indicated by the uninitiated clergy responding to the survey. We early on sought to create a litany of descriptive words for each of the three categories of clergy, and the list looked something like this. Priest/Catholic = Father, liturgy, sacraments,

Eucharist, confession, absolution, divine economy; Scholar/Lutheran = Doctor, sermon, Luther, scripture, spokesperson, theology, worldly knowledge; and Pastor/Methodist = friend, counselor, social, involved, community, issues, congregation. Again, the Episcopalians constituted the uncertain. The categories were simple, almost simple-minded, but nevertheless effective in the design of the questions.

THE QUESTIONNAIRE ... Getting Real Information from Real People

Sociologists call this the "research instrument," and it is the most crucial component of a data-based study, for it is the mechanism by which data are generated. And without data, there is no study, and with no data, there is nothing left but to surmise and speculate, wandering the aisles in search of that, which only by actually asking, can one expect to find. We may not like what we hear, but if we ask questions we will get answers.

In terms of structure, the questionnaire followed fairly standard format and style. There were four categories of questions broken down into (1) Biographical Data, which included such things as age, gender, ethnicity, years in the ministry, academic degrees, denominational affiliation, and a call for the respondents to rank in order of importance their own self-image from the three descriptive terms -- scholar, priest, pastor; (2) Scholarly Functions; (3) Priestly Functions; and (4) Pastoral Functions. The physical layout of the questionnaire allowed for it to be printed on both sides of a standard 8 1/2" x 11" sheet of typing paper including an introduction explaining the nature of the study. A self-addressed stamped envelope was also included, and four thousand clergy were in the data base.

Each of the three categories of clergy function -- scholar, priest, pastor -- had five specific activities. Accompanying each of these five activities were three simple charts -- one asking for the number of hours a week spent engaged in each activity with a chart allowing for from one to ten hours a week for each activity, another asking the clergy to indicate in their own view the value the parish placed upon each activity on a scale of one to five, with one being low and five being high, and a third chart asking the clergy to rank the value of each activity using the same low to high ranking system. Thus, each of the fifteen activities (five in each of three categories of scholar, priest, and pastor) involved three separate charts -- one for hours, another for parish valuation, and the third for clergy valuation.

These three categories were identified in the study by formal titles and their accompanying initials. The hourly chart has been labeled *Time Task Allocation* or TTA; the parish valuation chart is called the *Parish Task Valuation Assessment* or PTVA; and the clergy valuation chart is called the *Clergy Task Valuation Assessment* or CTVA. Some analytical rules were established in light of the quantity and quality of the data generated. Two rules were established. First, in the TVA (Task Valuation Assessment) chart, when the respondent marked the valuation of the activity either 1 or 2, the data were considered to reflect a low valuation and, when marked a 4 or 5, the data were believed to reflect a high valuation. If the activity received a 3 ranking, the data were thought to be indifferent as an indication of valuation (this simple rule applied to both Task Valuation Assessment charts, i.e., for the parish as well as for the clergy). Second, the Time Task Allocation chart was interpreted to indicate a low priority if falling between 1 and 3 hours and high if between 8 and 10, with an indifferent reading for hours 4 thru 7.

The intent was to identify "stress" areas in the ministry brought on by conflict between parish and pastor. We were also eager to identify "satisfaction" areas as well. The criterion employed in assessing stress-inducing situations was if there existed a striking imbalance of approval/disapproval for any given activity between parish and pastor such that the approval/disapproval ranking fell within the low or high classification then a stress-inducing situation existed. Activities which received indifferent rankings were discounted as irrelevant to our analysis. So, when the Task Value Assessment chart is off balance, then stress is generated, and when it is in balance, whether low or high, then satisfaction is generated. A simple listing of the various options was developed to serve as a quick reference:

When TTA and PTVA are high and CTVA is low.....then stress results.
When TTA and CTVA are high and PTVA is low.....then stress results.
When TTA and PTVA are low and CTVA is high.....then stress results.
When TTA and CTVA are low and PTVA is high.....then stress results.
When TTA is low and PTVA and CTVA are high.....then stress results.
When PTVA is low and TTA and CTVA are high.....then stress results.
When CTVA is low and TTA and PTVA are high.....then stress results.
When TTA is high and PTVA and CTVA are low.....then stress results.
When PTVA is high and TTA and CTVA are low.....then stress results.

When CTVA is high and TTA and PTVA is low.......then stress results.

When TTA, CTVA, and PTVA are in balance (low or high), satisfaction results.

The three categories for analysis -- scholar, priest, pastor -- each carried five specifically identified activities. There was a great deal of time spent selecting these particular activities, and, obviously, the list could have been longer. Actually, at one point, over one hundred individually identified activities of ministry were in the running for inclusion. Finally, reason prevailed, namely, everything could not be included, so we selected the five in each category which consistently received approval by our pre-test survey. For the record, we will recite all of the activities here under each categorical name -- scholar, priest, pastor.

SCHOLAR   (1) Preparing the Sunday homily or sermon.
           (2) Studying/reading major theologians of the day.
           (3) Systematic, regular exegetical study of scripture.
           (4) Serving as a spokesperson of authority for the teachings of the church.
           (5) Functioning as a valued and respected intellectual within the life of the parish.

PRIEST   (1) Leading the congregation in public worship.
           (2) Presiding over the Eucharist/Communion/Lord's Supper.
           (3) Exercising "sacramental" functions of ministry such as hearing confessions, baptizing, absolutions, anointing the sick, etc. (excluding from this time frame Eucharistic celebrations).
           (4) Functioning as a Spiritual Director to members of the parish.
           (5) Exercising discipline according to the canons of the church including counseling as relates to discipline.

PASTOR   (1) Involved in individual and family pastoral counseling sessions.
           (2) Involved in social activities within the life of the parish itself.
           (3) Involved in social activities within the life of the outside community.

(4) Addressing within the public forum social, moral, and political issues of the day within the life of the community.

(5) Serving the administration of the parish's life and that of the diocese.

Subsequent to the gathering and plotting of the data, the analysis was divided into two distinct arenas. First, the "indigenous" data was considered, namely an analysis of data gathered from within each of the four denominations without particular reference to the other denominations during the analysis process. So, for example, when we were doing the indigenous analysis of the Methodist data we stayed within the confines of that data base and did not reach across to compare the data with the Lutheran or Catholic data. However, after a thorough-going analysis of the indigenous data (Chapter Three), we then moved aggressively into the comparative analysis (Chapter Four) which allowed us to reach across denominational lines for some rather interesting comparisons and contrasts in our findings. We were particularly interested in comparing and contrasting stress-inducing situations within each of the four traditions in search of explanations which might be relevant to all.

CHAPTER THREE

INDIGENOUS ANALYSIS
Denominational Integrity in Task-Time Assessments
(summaries of all data categories within each tradition)

Eventually, one has to go to the empirical data to make the analysis which has been proposed in the foregoing discussion. Therefore, in this chapter, we will engage the data in each of the four denominations being treated here with initial interest in the overall averages of all of the categories under examination. In the following chapter we will venture into the dangerous and troubling, though ever so inviting and stimulating, wonderland of comparative analysis. That must come after we have maintained denominational integrity by staying within each tradition for the thorough recitation of the findings and a careful analysis of their implications. As we have done throughout this study, the order of treatment will be Methodist, Lutheran, Catholic, and Episcopal.

METHODIST
(BIOGRAPHICAL DATA (Age/Gender/Ethnicity/Academic Training)

The average age of the respondents for this national study does not necessarily represent the average age of all those in the ordained ministry of the United Methodist church, though, as we have argued earlier, we must assume that our numbers are rather close to the national average in all categories based on the size and random distribution of our survey sample. The average age, then, for Methodist clergy studied herein, is forty-six years of age. Eighty percent were men and of those, only four percent were self-identified as minority. Furthermore, only thirty-two percent had taken an advanced degree beyond that required for ordination, and of those who had taken advanced degrees, nearly ninety percent (88%) had taken the Doctor of Ministry degree.

SELF-IMAGE IN MINISTRY

We have suggested earlier in this study that, at least in terms of the tradition's own history, expectations would be high that Methodist clergy would be expected to define themselves and their ministries primarily in terms of "pastoral" functions and duties, and much less likely to define themselves in either the intellectual or sacerdotal role of ministry. Our expectations were confirmed because ninety percent of the Methodist clergy indicated that they thought of themselves first and foremost as "Pastor" rather than "Priest," with only four percent claiming this as their primary self-definition and, likewise, only four percent thought of themselves as primarily a "Scholar" in ministry. In the final analysis, Methodist clergy claimed "Pastor" as their fundamental characteristic.

SCHOLARLY FUNCTIONS

In this category of data, we have earlier indicated that five major tasks are to be characterized as "scholarly" in the sense that the intellectual commitment of the clergy must be to the fore in the exercise and discharge of these five functions, viz., preparing the sermon, the study of theology and scripture, acting as an informed, authoritative, and learned voice on behalf of the church, and being perceived as and acting in the capacity of, an intellectual within the life of the faith-community itself. Naturally, individual personalities and community preferences must always be factored in and taken account of, but the following summaries will, nevertheless, indicate where both the "satisfaction" and the "stress" indicators are to be found in the Methodist church today.

In our earlier discussion of methodology in Chapter Two, we outlined how we would be classifying the data on the basis of "stress" and "satisfaction" indicators so that we might more readily identify clergy tasks which contribute to one or the other characteristic. In the following, we will use abbreviations for our analysis to avoid laborious repetition of lengthy categorical terms. The first one will be TTA, by which, as discussed in Chapter Two, we mean the "Time Task Allocation," that is to say, on a scale of one hour to ten hours, the clergy indicate how many hours they give to particular task and how many hours they think their congregation thinks the clergy should give to that same task. Here, naturally, we are looking for divergences in valuation. This leads to the other two categorical terms, namely, CTVA, by which we mean "Clergy Task Value Assessment," and PTVA, by which we mean "Parish Task Value Assessment."

As noted earlier in our discussion of this method of analysis, we have decided that a low valuation will be given to tasks requiring three hours or less and a high valuation for those requiring or receiving eight or more hours. The middle hours are dismissed as not indicating significant valuation either way. So, a typical summary of a given task, say, "mowing the lawn," might read something like this -- the TTA is 2.5 hours weekly with the CTVA being low and the PTVA being high. This particular example, fortunately, was not in the survey, but for illustrative purposes let us deal with the data given here. The suggestion that the pastor values the time spent mowing the lawn as low, whereas the congregation thinks that task and the allocation of time for that purpose to be of great importance, will, we propose, lead to a "stress-inducing" situation because, as discussed earlier, stress is generated whenever there is an *imbalance* in the valuations placed on time allocations between that of the congregation and that of the clergy.

The "Task Value Assessment" is allocated to both the clergy (CTVA) and the parish (PTVA). We have chosen to suggest that "high importance" is placed on a task when the category "clergy" or "parish" reaches sixty percent(60%) in valuation and "low importance" when it falls below forty percent(40%). We have chosen to discard responses falling between forty(40%) and sixty(60%) percent as inconclusive of preference, as was established for the Time Task Allocation time frame between four and seven hours. This has been discussed and illustrated in detail in Chapter Two but a quick reminder of the analytical method seems helpful at this juncture, just as we are about to begin the summary report on all data gathered. The reader might refresh memory by a quick reread of the relevant passages in Chapter Two on "Categories and Itemized Variables" and "Analytical Rules -- TTA/PTVA/CTVA."

In the master category of "Scholarly Functions" of ministry, Methodist clergy spend an average of 6.5 hours weekly on sermon preparation. This has received a 72% high valuation by the parish as the pastor perceives it and an 80% high valuation by the clergy themselves.

However, in the category dealing with the studying and reading of major theologians of the day, the average pastor spends only 2.25 hours weekly on this activity and perceives parish approval of this small amount of time at 92%, with some 44% of the clergy in concurrence with this parish valuation and only 18% indicating a high valuation placed on the study of contemporary theology. The contrast between the high valuation placed by both parish and pastor on sermon preparation is further complemented by a low valuation placed on reading theology.

We find a significant divergence, however, between parish and pastor valuation when we come to the study of scripture, for while the average clergy spends 3.75 hours weekly in the exegetical study of scripture, 48% of the parish indicate a low valuation of this activity, whereas 62% of the clergy place a high valuation on such study. Thus, by using our stress-inducing indicator of high/low imbalance in Task Value Assessment between parish and pastor, we must conclude that there is evident stress in the average pastor's life and the average parish of the Methodist church when it comes to the amount of time given to, and the valuation of, the study of scripture on the part of the pastor. Staying with our 40% - 60% category as indicating insignificance, we find that 48% of the parish and only 14% of the pastors think the study of scripture of low importance, whereas we find that only 20% of the parish and 62% of the clergy think that task of high importance.

When we then come to an assessment of the pastor serving as a spokesperson of authority for the teachings of the church, we find the average clergy spending only 2.5 hours weekly in such functions with 52% of the parish and 46% of the clergy themselves placing a low valuation on this type of activity. When percentages are closely aligned, whether low (as with 28% of the parish and 20% of the clergy indicating a low importance to sermon preparation) or high (as in this instance of 52% parish and 46% clergy valuing the pastor as an authoritative spokesperson), we find this to be a "satisfaction" indicator. On the other hand, when we find major imbalances in the percentages (as with 48% of the parish indicating low valuation to scripture study and the clergy at 62% indicating high valuation), we find a ready-made situation for "stress" induction. Throughout each of the denominational assessments we will be on watch for "satisfaction"-inducing and "stress"-inducing indicators, always expecting "imbalance" of percentages, whether low or high, to be our tell-tale sign of problems.

Finally, in the "Scholarly Functions" category, we find that the average pastor spends about 3.75 hours weekly discharging functions as a respected intellectual within the life of the parish, with some 42% of the parish thinking this of low importance, whereas 42% of the clergy think it of high importance. Again, using our rule of imbalance, we must conclude that within the Methodist church today, this is a source of stress for the clergy, viz., desiring to function in the role of intellectual within the faith-community while that same community thinks little of that function.

PRIESTLY FUNCTIONS

The second grouping of activities and functions are classified as having to do with the role of the clergy as a "Priest" within the faith-community. This description was discussed earlier in Chapter Two, so a mere reminder of its meaning is needed here. The priestly functions of the clergy are categorized into five identifiable activities, namely, (1) the leading of public worship, (2) presiding over Holy Communion, (3) discharging functions of ministry that are defined as "sacramental," yet other than Communion, (4) functioning as a spiritual director or advisor to members of the congregation, and, finally, (5) exercising discipline by way of enforcing the canons of the denomination on errant members of the community.

The first category of activity in the priestly role we have identified is that of the leader of public worship for the congregation. Satisfaction between the parish and the pastor in the Methodist tradition is extremely high according to our findings, with 90% of the faith-community and 80% of the clergy indicating that this is of high importance in the activities of the pastor's life and function within the parish. We would naturally anticipate a high importance placed by both pastor and parish on this function and would, indeed, anticipate such an emphasis in all four traditions under consideration here. It would prove interesting, but far outside the purview of this study, to investigate those faith-communities in which such a function would not be so easily identified or valued. One might speculate and invite either corroborating evidence or justified criticism in suggesting that possibly, at least within the Christian tradition, this function might not be assessed as so very important within the unprogrammed meetings of the Religious Society of Friends known as Quakers, and, possibly, the Unitarian church might feel somewhat akin to the Quakers on this point as well. These unguarded remarks might, one would hope, lead to such a study by those more knowledgeable about these and similar communities of faith, with an eye towards a deeper understanding of their view of the nature and role of ministry leadership where "priestly" functions are not so obviously evidenced nor nurtured.

Whereas the Methodist pastor has indicated in the above category that three hours a week are spent in leading public worship, in the instance of Holy Communion ("Eucharist" the more common term in Catholic circles), the Methodist pastor spends only about one hour a week and, in obvious contrast to the high approval rating of time allocations by the parish and clergy in matters of public worship, only 38% of the parish but 74% of the clergy place a high importance valuation on presiding at Holy Communion. Without doubt, there is a major problem of perceived importance here between the clergy and the laity. Because of the striking imbalance in the percentages, we quite decidedly have a "stress-inducing" situation here on the Methodist scene. Again, whereas 32% of parishioners indicate a low importance on this function, only 14% of the clergy feel so. Thus, there are actually two stress-inducing conflicts uncovered in this category, that is, between the pastor (74% say highly important) and the parish (only 38% indicating a high value on the function), as well as within the faith-community itself, with 38% saying highly important and 32% indicating to the contrary. With one in three members of the congregation saying presiding at Holy Communion is of high value and one in three saying it is of low value, needless to say, there is a fundamentally different perception of this priestly function which must certainly manifest itself in the general life of the parish.

Because Catholic clergy spend over eight hours weekly in the celebration of Eucharist, one might be amused with the contrast in the numbers, i.e., the Methodist clergy say at an astounding rate of 74% that presiding at the Lord's Table is of high value, yet spend only one hour a week at that function. One must, therefore, be quickly reminded here that the sacramental emphasis within the Methodist tradition varies considerably from that of the Catholic church such that a bit of time spent in this function does not fairly represent the real importance placed on its function within the life of the parish or as evidenced in the self-definition of the clergy's role in matters of worship. One might readily be led into a surmise which can only be validated or disproven by an empirical study of yet-to-be-gathered data, to the effect that the

Methodist laity are less "sacramentally insistent" in their community-sense of worship than are their clergy. One is almost led to say the Methodist clergy are more "catholic" in the sense of "sacramentality" than are their laity. Certainly Methodist bishops and superintendents, to say nothing of Methodist theologians and church leaders, must take full account of this major stress-inducing conflict regarding Holy Communion in the overall life of the community of faith.

Using our rule of 40% - 60% being inconclusively indicative of strong feelings either high or low, we are led to believe that, whereas there is a great deal of stress-inducing conflict latent within the pastor-parish relationship over the place of Holy Communion in the life of the parish and the pastor's time allocated to it, we must conclude that in all other functions of ministry, excepting Holy Communion, there is a general concensus, at least between the parish (36% of whom place a high importance on those functions) and the pastor (40% of whom concur). However, between two significant blocks of parishioners there is a major conflict, with 36% indicating a high valuation on these functions and 38% indicating low to those same functions. Again, and interestingly, nearly forty percent (38%) of the parish indicate a low valuation on these functions and just over twenty percent (22%) of the clergy feel the same way. From a perspective of priestly functions, one might be a bit taken aback by the large percentage of the Methodist clergy (38%) who feel the non-Eucharistic functions of ministry are neither high nor low in importance. The appearance of indifference to matters of ministry function identified in this category, viz., baptisms, confessions, anointing the sick, etc., may be thought of in keeping with the lower sense of "sacramentalism" as relates to ministry function in evidence among the Methodist clergy who appear to greatly value other functions of ministry such as preaching and the study of scripture.

Satisfaction levels for clergy and the parish are rather high when it comes to the consideration of the priestly role of "spiritual director." Methodist clergy report spending an average of 4.5 hours a week in this ministry, with only 16% of the congregation and only 10% of the clergy indicating a low valuation on this function. In contrast, there is an outstanding 42% of the congregation along with 64% of the clergy who place a high valuation on this role. In an earlier day not really so long ago, this information would have been considered rather surprising if not downright alarming, for, historically, "spiritual direction" as such has been specifically a function of the Catholic clergy and those in religious vocations such as nuns and monks. Talk of such things within Protestant circles would have been thought quite alien.

However, during the last fifteen years, there has been a major burst of interest in spirituality and all things related to its place in pastoral ministry within the ranks of Protestant clergy. Indeed, many Protestant seminaries today are beginning to offer courses in spirituality and spiritual direction as a rightful topic of concern and activity for those training for the ordained ministry. What is even more refreshing is the large number of Protestant laity who have taken up the gauntlet and have begun to demand of their churches instruction in this field of learning. For centuries the Catholic church has placed major emphasis upon this function of ministry and the parishes across the land are replete with clergy, religious, and laity all functioning in the role of spiritual directors, but to find the Methodist parish and clergy valuing this role is indicative of the opening up within Protestantism itself to the winds of change which have swept out of Rome and through the ranks of the postconciliar movement of Vatican II.

Finally, as regards priestly functions of ministry, we find a strikingly poignant instance of stress-inducing conflict over the role of disciplinarian within the ministry of the Methodist church. Without attempting to identify those canons which call for enforcement within the community of faith by the clergy, the survey asked the clergy to indicate the amount of time spent in discharging this function and to report the perceived value placed on such activities by the parish. Just over one hour per week is spent in such matters, the clergy report and only 2% of the parish, while 28% of the clergy, think this is an activity of high importance. With nearly fifteen times as many clergy as laity valuing this activity highly, this is a major arena for inducing stress and conflict. Furthermore, 82% of the laity and only 44% of the clergy say this is a low priority for clergy time, giving rise to yet another spin on this very troubling time-allocation conflict within the Methodist church.

Is discipline important or not? And if so, who is to say? Obviously the laity do not think so while nearly half of the clergy believe it is. Again, an understanding of this situation might be greatly aided with attention being called to the "Protestant" nature of the problem and the "Protestant" nature of the response. That is to say, the existence and application of authority within the Protestant tradition has always been a major point of conflict and discussion since, one might surmise, the emergence of Protestantism itself. Certainly one must see Luther's Theses as a beginning in what was to eventuate into a pervasive spirit of challenge to the Catholic sense of *Magisterium*.

The implicit problem within this sense of justified challenge to church authority is the obvious difficulty in establishing a standard to which all would agree. In the absence of the Magisterium and, today, with the decline in any real sense of confidence (owing to the emergence of form criticism) in the notion of *sola Scriptura*, the laity of the Protestant Churches seem to be in a quandary as to the final source of discipline, excepting in the fundamentalist churches, where a perceived right of each believer to establish dogma and practice individually exists. With these strikingly alarming numbers indicating deep differences within the Methodist community of faith between clergy perceptions and laity perceptions, leaders of the denomination would be well-advised to address the issue of authority and discipline in the church without delay, even if to say nothing more than that there is not and may not be and should not be a standard of authority for discipline. If such a position is in keeping with the Methodist tradition established by the Wesley brothers, who themselves profoundly challenged the Anglican church of their day, then to make such a statement and take such a stand would, in the final analysis, be of major pastoral benefit to the community of faith.

PASTORAL FUNCTIONS

If major conflicts exist between parish and pastor over the exercise of authority and discipline within the church which has been defined in this study as a "priestly function," then one is not surprised to find a reasonable level of agreement regarding the "pastoral function" of counseling. We recall from our opening remarks on the data regarding Methodist clergy that they and their congregations define their ministry fundamentally and primarily in "pastoral" terms rather than either as a "scholar" or as a "priest." In this third category of data, "Pastoral Functions," we will consider five distinct areas of activity and assess the pastor's time and valuation and that of the parish. These five areas include (1) pastoral counseling, (2) involvement within the social life of the parish, (3) involvement within the social life of the community itself outside of the parish as such, (4) dealing with social/moral/political issues of the day as relevant within the life of the community, and, finally, (5) a consideration of the time spent and valuation placed upon the necessary administrative requirements and responsibilities implicit within the exercise of ministry as defined by the Methodist church.

Whereas the exercise of discipline is a major point of stress between pastor and parish, the exercise of pastoral counseling is not. The average pastor spends about four hours a week in this ministry function and 40% of the congregation and 54% of the clergy believe time spent in this activity is of high importance. Though only 16% of the clergy place a low valuation on pastoral counseling, a surprising 36% of the parish so rate this ministry. It is informative, indeed, to see that better than one in three members of an average Methodist parish places a low valuation on pastoral counseling given the undisputed "pastoral" nature of that ministry.

What is even more insightful is the fact that more of the laity believe "spiritual direction" to be of higher importance than "pastoral counseling." Something is obviously going on here worthy of our investigation. In only four other areas of activity, viz., sermon preparation (72%), leading public worship (90%), serving as spiritual director (42%), and addressing social issues (68%), do we have a higher percentage of the laity allocating a high importance rating to a ministry function than we do in the exercise of pastoral counseling. Just over half (54%) of the clergy place a high value on pastoral counseling, but, again, 64% of the clergy placed a high value on spiritual direction. A full ten percent of the clergy believe spiritual direction to be more important than pastoral counseling.

What could be going on here? What must cause us to pause and evaluate our situation are the complexities and varieties of present forms of ministry being "offered" to the laity and the types of ministry which the laity are choosing to "accept." Offering a ministry and having that ministry accepted are two related, but quite different things. Could it be that laity today are calling for a more "spiritual" ministry from their pastor which they see to be more in keeping with the pastor's role, while a "counseling" ministry is seen as more in keeping with the health-providing industry of the wider community? It's just a question, but it keeps popping up time and time again when congregations of worshiping people indicate a disinclination to foster counseling in the parish but a genuine interest in fostering spiritual direction.

Dr. William B. Oglesby, Jr., former founding President of the Association of Clinical Pastoral Education, once said he feared that "pastoral counseling" as a profession would be the last great haven for the clergy who had lost their faith in Christ and His church but who still wanted to serve people. He indicated in an address at the Graduate Theological Foundation in Indiana, that he expected the field of spiritual direction within the Protestant churches to eventually take the place of pastoral counseling in parish ministry. "People want to pray, and read the Bible, and talk about their faith," he said in speaking of the laity, "and too often the pastoral counselor is in the throes of a personal crisis of faith and commitment to the church, which makes such talk problematic." And once more, as we have seen above in several areas such as in the non-Eucharistic functions of ministry, we sense a real division within the laity over this issue of pastoral counseling, with four in ten saying it is important and nearly that same proportion (36%) saying it is not. Here, again, we may sense a difference of perceived needs by the laity -- some wanting spiritual direction with an emphasis on the spiritual and the rest wanting pastoral counseling with an emphasis on the counseling.

Though the issue of pastoral counseling seems not to be a stress-inducing area for the clergy, the issue of social involvement within the life of the parish is quite decidedly a significant stress inducer. While the clergy indicate they spend an average of four and a quarter hours a week discharging such responsibilities, 68% of the parish approve of such high importance placed on this function, while 32% of the clergy disapprove. Only 10% of the laity disapprove. This constitutes a massive gap in the perception of ministry -- nearly seven in ten parishioners approve of their pastor spending time engaged in social activities in the congregation, while better than three in ten clergy say it is unimportant.

Only in the areas of the study of scripture, Holy Communion, discipline, and (as we shall see later) social issues and administration have we seen such a wide degree of separation between the clergy and the laity in their ranking of ministry priorities. In every instance listed thus far, excepting this one, we find the clergy wanting to place much more emphasis upon those various functions -- study, Communion, discipline, social issues, administration -- and only in this category of the social life of the parish do we find the pastor disinclined, while the congregation is expectantly approving of more time in this pastoral activity. The three major categories of activities in which the congregation is ready to place a high priority on time spent by the clergy are (1) Preaching, (2) Public Worship, and (3) the Social Life of the Parish. To understand the disparity between what the clergy want to do with their time -- Study, Communion, Discipline, Social Issues, Administration -- and what the congregation wants emphasized, is the challenge of the day.

If the pastor and the parish are at odds over the valuation of allocated time for engaging in the social life of the parish, there is little measurable difference in their mutual dislike of spending time engaged in the social activities of the community outside of the parish. Only 18% of the laity and 22% of the clergy think such activity worthy of the pastor's time, while 54% of the parish and 38% of the clergy think it a waste of time. Few activities among Methodist clergy receive more affirmative support in their own feelings about ministry matters than do the issue of social activities within the wider community outside of the congregation. The pastor, it seems, is for the congregation and not to be in service to the community, spending, nevertheless, three hours a week on various community-based activities outside the parish. Such attitudes have historical roots but certainly the Anglican tradition from which the Wesley brothers came would not have fostered such feelings during the 18th century in England. During their time, the local parish pastor was thought of as the pastor to the village or town or city and not merely and solely to the local congregation. Today, the attitude has drastically changed. The pastor, according to these data, is not essentially the pastor to the town, but the pastor to the congregation. Better than five out of ten (54%) of the laity and nearly four out of ten (38%) of the clergy give a low rating to time spent in the wider community.

However, if spending time on social activities in the community outside the parish is mutually agreed upon as a waste of good time by both the pastor and the parish, such a satisfying agreement does not exist over the issue of addressing social, moral, and political issues of the day. Spending only two hours a week doing just that, only 10% of the congregation approve while 64% quite decidedly disapprove. On the other hand, 44% of the clergy think this is time well spent, with less than three in ten (28%) thinking it less important. Here we have a stress-inducing situation, to be sure. More than four times as many clergy as laity think this is time well spent and better than twice as many laity (64%) as clergy (28%) think it less than important.

An argument could be made that those in ministry have failed, in such an instance as this, in conveying to the faith-community the centrality of its religious beliefs and commitments to the issues facing the society in which it lives and serves. A community of faith which values extremely highly the preparation of sermons, the study of scripture, the leading of worship, and the providing of spiritual direction, but, at the same time, abjures discussion of social, political, and moral issues by the clergy, is in a state of denial of its mission unlike any such duplicity which might be tolerated in any other social institution. To call for preaching and teaching and spiritual guidance and refuse to address the moral issues of the day seems patently to fly in the face of the Protestant position regarding the centrality of the personal life of Jesus and the individual's very personal response to that life in ministering to the world.

Finally, and far from least, the Methodist clergy are in a major stress situation when it comes to the meaning and nature of administrative work for the denomination and the perception of that work by the congregation being served. In a world fraught with administrative red tape and at a time when Protestant denominations the country over find themselves in a retrenching posture regarding diminishing membership, aging real estate, and failures in marketing of growth efforts, it does not strike one as odd or incongruous that clergy are called upon to become more and more astute in management of property, personnel, and programs.

What does strike one as somewhat askew is the realization that parishioners are not interested in, nor supportive of, their clergy spending time managing the shop, i.e., taking care of the administrative functions needed and required by the denomination in order to stay in business. Nearly seven hours a week (6.75) are spent by the clergy on administrative procedures within their denominational judicatories. That constitutes nearly a whole day out of the five-day work week. Only 22% of the parish but a full 40% of the clergy think this is time well spent, i.e., it receives a high importance mark on the valuation chart. On the other hand, a full 40% of the parish but only 22% of the clergy feel it is of little importance, i.e., it receives a low mark for importance. Obviously, the clergy know something the parish does not know, or at least it appears so.

Is it possible that the Protestant notion of *sola Scriptura* and the necessity for the individual to "work out your own salvation" has led to a situation in which the laity are disinterested in the denomination as an administrative machine and only interested in matters related to personal faith such as sermons, scripture study, worship, spiritual direction, and the like? Could it be that the very genius of the "Protestant Principle," as Paul Tillich called it, has created an anti-establishment mentality on the part of the laity? This, of course, is certainly not characteristic of the clergy who find themselves team players in the management of the corporation. Or, is this being too harsh? Might it merely be that the laity, not having immediate access to the denominational machine, find themselves sufficiently insulated (not isolated) from the mechanism that makes the Methodist church functional and viable? Might they, instead, find themselves in a cocoon rather than perceiving themselves and their pastor as team players in the management operations of the denominational machine? Whereas clergy are taught to pledge allegiance to the denomination (thus three or four year tenures and then relocation within the superintendency), the laity think of the church as their local congregation and their faith as a very personal relationship with Jesus, having nothing particularly to do with institutional administration. This notion is so alien to the experience and practice of Catholic laity and clergy that the comparative stage of this study is, even now, calling us forward.

THE WORK WEEK

It is significant to note that Methodist clergy indicated that they average 52 hours a week working in the parish. This is, obviously, a full twelve hours above the normally accepted work week. The fact that this is reported by the clergy is, as we discussed in the opening pages of this book, not so much about truth and reality as about perceived truth and reality. Whether Methodist clergy normally and regularly spend 52 hours a week on the job is not the issue -- what is important for their own self-understanding is that they think they spend 52 hours a week on the job. Certainly, what it does indicate to us is that they are, by professional standards, overworked and, therefore, think of themselves as overworked. What this does to their self-image and their clear, balanced, and fair view of the world around them we are left to speculate.

Gone are the days when the clergy, those in positions of pastoral care and spiritual direction, found they had leisure, had time to "loaf and invite the soul," as Wordsworth called it. What this overworked ethos conveys to the parish is anyone's guess, but we might imagine a calmer, less hectic environment when clergy were free to enjoy the privilege of having time to think, to meditate, to contemplate the verities of life, and thereby grow spiritually and, in turn, be in a better position to offer spiritual guidance to those really in need of such. That clergy are merely overworked, exhausted hackers (or perceive themselves to be) is both sad and pathetic -- sad for those genuinely seeking spiritual guidance and pathetic for the clergy who find themselves in a work environment so demanding as to leave themselves feeling emotionally and physically spent. Much more needs to be said and done about this situation, but we will hold final comments on this point until this study has reached its full culmination.

STRESS-INDUCERS

The purpose for doing this study and writing this book, as mentioned at the outset, is to provide real information, i.e., empirical data, for those who are interested and in a position to address problems and offer solutions. What the world is desperately in need of at this particular time is not yet another speculative book on what might be wrong, what might possibly be done, what could conceivably be suggested, about the various and sundry issues related to the problematics of ministry. There are enough of such at Blackwell's Book Shop. What, however, might be of interest to those in positions of leadership, what might be helpful to those in positions of power and authority, is an actual collection of information based on real facts, actual evidence generated by those most concerned, namely, the clergy themselves. There is nothing quite like having factual information in the decision-making process.

We have not gotten all of the relevant information but we have gotten some of it, and what we have gotten is real, it's tangible, it's actually gathered from those who are directly involved and concerned. That is, we asked the clergy and they gave us answers to our questions. And what we have from the beginning been interested in are those situations which produce stress and those happy but selective situations which produce satisfaction. Then, on the basis of the real facts from real people in real situations, we are able to identify satisfying situations with the hope that those in positions of leadership will capitalize on them and seek to perpetuate them throughout the ministry. And for those situations which produce stress, we have attempted to identify them and characterize them such that those in leadership positions might work to create a work environment such where stress-inducing situations might be reduced or avoided in the future to the mutual benefit of clergy and parish.

Of fifteen areas of professional activity (divided into five areas for each of the scholar, priest, and pastor categories), seven have proven to be stress-inducers for the Methodist clergy. Immediately, this seems both high and problematic. Almost half of the professional activity categories are stressers for Methodist clergy where as eight are satisfaction inducers. Since stress factors are more easily identified than satisfaction factors, let us address these seven activities first and save the satisfaction activities until the end of this discussion. The seven stress-inducing activities are (1) the study of scripture, (2) functioning as an intellectual within the parish, (3) presiding at Holy Communion, (4) exercising discipline within the canons of the church's teachings, (5) being involved in the social activities of the parish, (6) addressing the social, moral, and political issues of the day, and (7) serving the administrative needs of the denomination.

Since we have already identified and commented on each of these in the above discussion, let us conclude this consideration of the Methodist clergy with just a few additional comments regarding each of these stress indicators. Obviously, Methodist clergy are at odds with their parish in terms of their personal desire to spend more time regularly and systematically studying scripture. Whereas the pastor thinks this important, the parish does not. Likewise, whereas the parish is not particularly interested in seeing their pastor function as a respected intellectual within the life of the parish, the pastor most decidedly wishes to do so. It is clear that there is a striking divergence of perceptions of the pastors' gifts and talents. In the 17th and 18th and almost through the 19th century, the pastor was quite clearly the most educated member of the typical village or town in America, but today it is the extremely exceptional pastor who is sufficiently educated in secular issues as to be respected by professional members of the parish as an intellectual equal. Too often, the pastor is merely tolerated as an "also ran" member of the intellegentsia within the parish.

Furthermore, Methodist clergy find themselves in a stress situation owing to the difference of opinion as to the relevance and place of Holy Communion within the parish, due to the fact that twice as many clergy as parishioners think of Communion as a major function of ministry. Even more extreme is the divergence of opinion as to the nature and role of discipline and the authoritative role of the church's teaching as applied to members of the parish. Virtually no Methodist laity believes the pastor should spend any time exercising discipline in matters of faith and practice. In such a situation and with such a low view of the church's responsibility regarding discipline and authority, little wonder the pastor finds stress mounting in the face of divergent life-styles and belief systems operative within the same community of faith. And, whereas most of the congregation believes the pastor should be involved in the social life of the community, hardly any believe the pastor should have anything to say about the social, moral, and political issues of the day. This juxtaposition of attitudes leaves the pastor in a bind, being asked to be socially active in the community but under no circumstances have anything to say about the issues facing society!

Finally, the pastor is between a rock and a hard place when it comes to spending time in service to the denomination because hardly any one in the parish believes time is well spent when discharging administrative functions. The pastor, on the other hand, is quite decidedly convinced of the importance of such functions and, therefore, finds stress mounting as time is spent on administration without support or encouragement from the parish.

SATISFACTION-INDUCERS

Satisfaction inducers are, of course, more enjoyable to discuss and more open to positive and adventurous explanation. We have already discussed in some detail the major categories of satisfaction for the clergy in their definition and function of ministry as reinforced by their congregations' concurrence about time-task allocations. Particularly, we have noted the presence of a mutually high approval of time spent in the areas of sermon preparation, the leading of public worship, pastoral counseling, and spiritual direction. It should be noted that the high approval ratings are divided up as follows— one is from the "scholarly" function list (sermon preparation), one is from the "pastoral" function list (pastoral counseling), and two are from the "priestly" function list (worship and spiritual direction).

Besides these four activities of mutually high satisfaction ratings between pastor and parish, there are several others which we have identified as fairly satisfying, by which we mean the pastor is more or less reaffirmed in the time allocation given to a particular task identified as of high importance to the individual pastor's own personal perception of ministry. Satisfaction comes, as we noted earlier in this study, when there is a close parity of valuation assessment between pastor and parish of a particular activity, whether that valuation is high or low. Other satisfying areas of pastoral ministry among the Methodist clergy identified in this study are (1) an agreement that the study of contemporary theologians is relatively unimportant, (2) that the pastor is not especially called upon to serve as a spokesperson of authority on the teachings of the church, and (3) that the pastor is not expected by the congregation to be involved in social activities in the community outside of the parish's own social life.

30   John H. Morgan

LUTHERAN

BIOGRAPHICAL DATA   (Age/Gender/Ethnicity/Academic Training)

The average age of the Lutheran clergy in this study was forty-eight years of age and all but 2% were men.   All but 4% were White and mostly Anglo-European.

Only 38% of the Lutheran clergy held an advanced degree in a cognate field of theology or ministry and of that number, less than half (42%) held a doctor's degree, mostly, but not exclusively, the Doctor of Ministry. In an earlier section of this study, it was suggested that historically the Lutheran clergy had been thought to be more rigorously trained in the intellectual aspects of ministry -- theology, history, scripture -- with a heavy emphasis upon the scholarly role of the pastor in the community. The low percentage of Lutheran clergy taking advanced degrees, particularly doctoral degrees, must, therefore, cause us to modify our expectations along these lines. The disappointing number of women clergy and minority clergy responding to this national survey gives one pause, leading one to wonder why the failure to participate in a randomly generated and executed study which was not denominationally sponsored. The study's independence from denominational alignment should have stifled any "in-house" fears or perceptions of hidden agendas or institutional bias. Speculative surmises as to causes are legion and we will not dally here to engage in the fun. Yet, speculate and surmise we will, none the less.

SELF-IMAGE IN MINISTRY

From the outset, we were determined to identify certain categories of ministry function which could easily and without much debate be separated out in terms of three major functional categories, viz., scholar, priest, and pastor. This was an attempt on our part to see if both the clergy and their respective denominations follow along similar lines of category identification. We were not disappointed in discovering that the Methodist clergy do, indeed, perceive themselves and are reinforced in that perception by their congregations, as essentially and fundamentally "pastors" to their communities of faith. However, in the Lutheran church, we have found a similar, though not an exact replica, of those sentiments and perceptions evidenced among the Methodists. When asked to rank in order of importance one's own personal ministry using the three possible categories of Scholar, Priest, or Pastor, 90% of the Lutheran clergy defined themselves as Pastor. The remaining 10% equally divided themselves as either "Scholar" or "Priest."

Edward Banfield at Harvard once observed, when it came to classifying oneself as in poverty or not, that "saying it makes it so." One is reminded of these words when we ask the clergy to characterize themselves, limiting them to only three words. In an earlier time we would have been more surprised than we are today to find that hardly any Protestant clergy define themselves as "scholar," rather preferring the more parish-oriented description of "pastor." The rather low frequency use of the "priest" classification is not surprising, however, and possibly only in the church of England and in the Episcopal church U.S.A. would we expect to find "non-Catholic" clergy using this term to define their ministries. Obviously, all Orthodox clergy are priests but, for our purposes, fall outside the scope of this study. Whether or not scholarship is considered by parish and/or pastor as important must be determined in our following discussion of the Lutheran clergy. We found that with the Methodist clergy, sermon preparation and the study of scripture were highly regarded (scripture study being esteemed much higher, however, by the Methodist clergy than by the Methodist laity) but the study of contemporary theology or serving as the intellectual spokesperson for the faith-community was valued rather low by Methodist clergy and laity alike. In the Lutheran tradition of "herr-professor-doctor-pastor," we must be more watchful for tell-tale signs of scholarship being valued more highly, possibly, than among the Methodist given the Lutheran tradition of German scholarship.

As discussed earlier in Chapter Two and again reiterated in the above consideration of the Methodist clergy, we will be seeking out stress-inducing situations and satisfaction-inducing situations in definitions and functions of ministry. We will take note of the actual clock time spent in any particular activity (called Time-Task Allocation or TTA) and we will take note of the parish's valuation of that particular activity (called the Parish Task Valuation Assessment or PTVA), as well as noting the corollary valuation placed on that same activity by the pastor (called the Clergy Task Valuation Assessment or CTVA). Again, we will consider any activity as valuated high when it receives a sixty percent (60%) or more approval rating from clergy and/or parish and low when its approval rating falls below forty percent (40%), with the reasonable suggestion that the middle twenty percent (40%-60%) proves inconclusive as an indicator of approval or disapproval.

Arguments are legion for different sets of criteria using differently constructed variables following alternative notions and conceptions of activities and priority-assessments. So be it. There is plenty of room for more than one study. However, these criteria, these categories, these sets of valuative tools have been chosen for this study and they will be employed with care and precision. This study, therefore, must be judged within the context of its own self-understanding and intentionality. Alien measures must not be used. Internal consistency and logical analysis are all that is sought here and this study must be measured against its own set of rules and stated purposes.

SCHOLARLY FUNCTIONS

Five different activities have been, as noted earlier, classified as of "scholarly" intent and character. There are many more and even some of these might arguably be placed elsewhere. But here, we will ascribe the classification "scholar" to the activities of (1) sermon preparation, (2) the study of theology, (3) the study of scripture, (4) the pastor serving as an authoritative spokesperson for the church's teachings, and (5) functioning within the parish as a respected intellectual.

Without question or doubt, the preparation of the Sunday sermon receives the greatest affirmation of importance for both the pastor and the parish in the Lutheran tradition. Seven hours a week, almost a full day out of the work week, is spent in preparing the homily and 86% of the parish and 88% of the clergy believe it to be of high importance in the function of ministry. The "Ministry of the Word" has, of course, been a major focus of the Lutheran tradition and the high level of parish/pastor affirmation of its primacy in the definition of ministry should be expected. Here, more so than in any other category of ministry activity, there is the highest level of satisfaction in the exercise of ministry as experienced by both the parish and the pastor. If we find troubling conflicts over the pastor's relationship with the outside community later in this investigation and if instances of stress-inducing conflict between pastor and parish turn up in other arenas, let it be noted here that a high-level mutuality of satisfaction is established in the area of time spent on sermon preparation in the Lutheran church.

When it comes to the study of contemporary theologians, the situation shifts drastically. The pastor spends only two and a half hours per week reading theology in the face of 88% of the parish who valuate such activity low in importance, accompanied by a surprising 44% of the clergy who feel likewise. Only one in three Lutheran pastors actually feels that the study of contemporary theology is important in the exercise of ministry. Though only half as many pastors as parishioners place a low valuation on reading theology, there is no reason to expect stress here because of the small percentage of pastors (30%) who actually place a high valuation on this activity.

Stress, however, emerges when we get to the study of scripture. This is really quite surprising given the historic emphasis placed on *sola Scriptura* by the mainline Protestant churches, and particularly the Lutherans. We found this same attitude among the Methodists (see above). Only three hours a week is given to the exegetical study of Scripture, just one-half hour longer than to the study of theology, but with only 22% of the congregation thinking this is of high importance in the exercise of ministry. More than twice that many parishioners (48%) actually give Scripture study a low rating on the valuation scale. The stress-producing situation comes when we discover that nearly three times (56%) as many pastors as parishioners give Scripture study a high rating, while nearly one-third as many pastors (18%) as parishioners (48%) give Scripture study an outright low rating. When there is such a wide-ranging spread as this in approval/disapproval rating of time allocation, stress is inevitable. One wonders what the parishioners think the pastor is to use in sermon preparation, an activity which is greatly treasured by the parish, if there is such a low estimation of the value of reading theology or studying Scripture! An interesting study is waiting to be conducted on the perception by the parish of how the pastor actually functions, particularly in such technical activities as sermon preparation, exegesis, and reading theology. If Scripture and theology are of low value while the sermon is of high value, where then comes the material? An interesting problem for the Lutheran clergy in educating the parish as to the importance of theology and Scripture in sermonizing is emerging from these findings.

Unlike the "satisfaction" indicated in the area of sermon preparation, the "satisfaction" indicated with regard to the pastor serving as a spokesperson of authority for the teachings of the church is rather passive or *laisse faire* in character. Two and three-quarter hours weekly are taken up in this activity and both the parish and the clergy seem to be more or less equally divided as to whether to give it a high or low rating. Because there is parity in the numbers on the part of pastors and congregations and nothing falling much outside the 40% to 60% range (which we classify as inconclusive), stress seems not to be induced in this ministry function. One in three parishioners (34%) and one in three pastors (32%) give the spokesperson's role a high valuation, but this is balanced by one in four (44%) parishioners and one in three (34%) pastors who give the same activity a low valuation of importance. Though stress seems not to be induced by this situation, using our established rules of stress-inducing criteria (see Chapter Two above), there does seem to be the possibility of stress within each group of parishes and pastors because the range is quite wide within each group between those who approve and those who disapprove. More or less one in three parishioners approve or disapprove of this activity and, likewise, more or less one in three pastors approve or disapprove. Obviously, there is a misperception or a deep-seated divergence of expectations regarding the nature of the pastor's role when it comes to serving as a spokesperson for the church's teaching. It is easier, one is led to observe, to understand the high approval rating of this activity than the low rating, for if the pastor is not to be the spokesperson for the teachings of the church, then who is?

A very similar ambiguity exists when we consider the pastor functioning as a valued and respected intellectual within the life of the parish. Surely this is a unique and recently evolved disparity within the Lutheran church in America. One would be hard pressed to convince this author that the Lutheran pastor in a typical German village or township in the 19th century would not have been thought of as a leading intellectual in the life of the congregation! To be sure, the same would certainly be verified by a look at the historic descriptions of Lutheran pastors in Scandinavia and North America as well, and not just during the 18th and 19th centuries, but certainly during the first half of the 20th century as well. What might one think in discovering that whereas the Lutheran pastor reportedly spends three and three-quarter hours weekly serving as a intellectual within the parish, less than one in three (28%) members of the congregation and just over one in three (34%) of the pastors think this is of high importance in the discharge of ministry, while better than one in three of both the parish (38%) and the clergy (36%) think it of low importance.

There is mutual satisfaction of a benign and passive sort here because the disparity does not fall into the stress-inducing range of dissatisfaction. One does wonder, however, as with the role of pastor as spokesperson, about the nature of the perception of ministry by the parish and the pastor when one in three members of the parish and one in three pastors give the intellectual role both a high and a low valuation. As we shall see, while sacramental ministries and spiritual direction receive high approval ratings on the one hand, on the other the pastor is not thought of as a significant representative of the intellectual life of the parish. What must be going on in this situation cries out for an answer, whether it has to do with a major shift in the historic self-understanding of Lutherans about the nature of ministry and the pastor's role in community, or whether it has merely been a failure on the part of clergy to keep their congregations instructed about the depth and nature of ministry training and function. *Satisfaction based on indifference* by either the parish or the pastor is hardly a positive situation in the long run and, in matters of the intellect in faith commitment, indeed, certainly cause for concern.

The first five categories of ministry activities we have characterized as "scholarly functions" for the reasons given above. Of these five areas, only one activity is responsible for creating stress, and that is over the difference of opinion between the parish and the pastor as to the relevance and significance of the study of scripture. Though we have been surprised by this, we, nevertheless, have identified the problem and reflected upon its meaning. One point is quite clear and quite at odds with our early "domain assumption" regarding the Lutheran tradition and the intellectual life, viz., the Lutheran church today in America does not seem to have defined itself consciously as primarily or predominantly a "scholarly" tradition but rather as a "pastoral" one.

PRIESTLY FUNCTIONS

In the following, we will identify and discuss five ministry activities characterized as "priestly" in nature. They are (1) the leading of public

36   John H. Morgan

worship, (2) presiding at the Eucharist, (3) exercising other "sacramental" ministries, (4) serving as a spiritual director, and (5) exercising discipline in accordance with the policies and practices of the church. Many others could have been identified, but these, it is felt, will give a feeling of the parish's and pastor's perceptions of ministry as "priestly" or not.

Aggressive and self-congratulatory levels of satisfaction for both the parish and the clergy are reached in an otherwise unprecedented fashion when it comes to approval of the pastor's role as the leader of public worship for the faith-community. Some 96% of the parish and 92% of the clergy concur in placing a high valuation on this function. Though only three hours a week are spent in discharging this responsibility (as compared to over eight hours for the Catholic priests), the expectation on the part of the parish regarding the pastor's rightful responsibility of worship leader is indisputably perceived to be the single most important ministry function of all, and the clergy agree. Only in the activity of presiding at the Eucharist do clergy give themselves a higher percentage of affirmation than they do for the leading of public worship. In fact, other than in sermon preparation, the clergy in no other category of activity reach a concensus beyond six in ten and average across the board in all categories of activity nearer to five in ten. If a pastor wishes to receive the approval of his peers and parish, then spend time conducting public worship and all will be well.

Only in presiding over Holy Communion do clergy reach a higher percentage of approval than they do for leading public worship. In presiding at Eucharist, better than nine in ten (94%) of the Lutheran pastors give a high valuation for their two hours a week discharging this function. Here, however, unlike the above category of public worship generally, the parish is less approving at just under eight in ten (78%) as opposed to nine in ten (96%) for public worship generally. That the Lutheran laity would make a distinction between "public worship" and "Holy Communion" at a rate of 16% is somewhat surprising given the increased emphasis upon the Sacrament of Holy Communion being encouraged by the Lutheran church today, at least among the clergy and Lutheran theologians. This may reflect, therefore, that inevitable and, one might suggest, universal phenomenon of the church's clergy leading out ahead of the church's laity.

Within Lutheran clerical circles today, the celebration of Eucharist has become the single most important function of the clergy's definition of their ministry (94% of the clergy can't be wrong!). This certainly would not have been the case even fifty years ago and one can consult the history books on Lutheran liturgical practice to learn that such an emphasis upon Holy Communion was not universally welcomed nor internationally represented. But today, and certainly in the United States, there is this broad feeling among Lutherans, particularly the clergy, but in ever-increasing numbers among the laity, for the centrality of the Eucharist. For the more Protestant-leaning Lutherans, this has not been universally welcomed but, for the more Catholic-leaning Lutherans, it seems only another step towards positive relations with the Roman Catholic church. In a word, the level of mutual "satisfaction" in the valuation of time allocation on the part of clergy and the parish could not be higher. Those meager 4% laity who place a low valuation on the clergy presiding at Holy Communion will naturally become increasingly alienated or will succumb inevitably to corrective instruction in matters of faith.

If the "sacramental function" of presiding at Holy Communion is outstandingly approved by clergy and laity alike, a bit less jubilant affirmation of other "sacramental functions of ministry" such as confessions, baptisms, absolutions, anointings, etc., is forthcoming. Though a half-hour a week more (2.5) is spent in these ministries than in presiding at Eucharist, just over six in ten of the laity (64%) and likewise of the clergy (64%), offer a high valuation for such activities with only one in ten of the parish and only 4% of the clergy valuing such ministries as low in importance. Even here we see a level of satisfaction which is gratifying, for of the eight categories of ministry activities considered thus far among the Lutherans, only one, i.e., the study of Scripture, has been defined as a stress-inducing situation. This positive trend will continue with only three rather striking and troubling exceptions.

In these areas of "sacramental functions of ministry," other than presiding at Eucharist, one will anticipate that as the Lutheran church continues as it is now, rather aggressively affirming its "Catholicity" in faith and practice, these percentages will continue to rise in approval ratings. The postconciliar "Re-Catholicization" of Lutheranism is certainly a topic fraught with heat as well as light, but is, nevertheless, one which is destined to occupy a significant place on the ecumenical agenda in the 21st century. It is becoming increasingly clear that the Lutheran tradition is asserting priority over Anglicans in dialogue with Rome and this self-conscious movement towards the "sacramentalization" of Lutheran ministry is merely another sign of this massive movement. That it is occurring in North America at an astounding rate should be of significance to those researchers wishing to identify empirically the relevant data characterizing this movement. With the Episcopal church in the U..S.A. losing its momentum in dialogue with Rome owing to a variety of issues, problems, and conflicting agendas, the Lutheran church is quite decisively taking the lead.

Only activities related to worship -- the sermon, leading public worship, presiding at Eucharist -- receive higher approval ratings than do that of the pastor functioning as a spiritual director. Better than six in ten (64%) of the parish, and likewise (66%) of the clergy, render a high valuation on this activity, with only one in ten pastors and just over two in ten (24%) members of the parish venturing a low rating for spiritual direction. This is certainly in keeping with our earlier discussion of the "Catholic" leaning of the American Lutheran community. Spiritual Direction has not, until very recently, even been on the seminary curriculum listing of required courses for clergy at Lutheran seminaries. Today that is all changed. Not only Lutheran, but most of the mainline Protestant seminaries, are introducing a full range of courses in spirituality, spiritual direction, and spiritual formation, many not only teaching the Catholic classics in spiritual theology, but some even offering practical training workshops in the actual practice of spiritual direction and spiritual formation.

This kind of talk, and even the use of this nomenclature only a few years ago, would have brought down the wrath of the Lutheran community upon any clergy venturing into these long uncharted waters. That the Lutherans threw away "far too much" in the Reformation is agreed universally (only some branches of the fundamentalists hold out on this point), and today there is an outright effort to "reclaim" that which was lost unnecessarily. One need only venture into a "Catholic" Lutheran church on a Sunday morning to quickly read the trend. The liturgy and the sacramentals of the church, the building and Sunday School curriculum, as well as the sermon and demeanor of those at worship and those presiding, all witness quite clearly to what is afoot. That spiritual direction as a major function of Lutheran ministry is supported by a large majority of parishioners and pastors alike, gives every evidence of this trend. And it has just begun. More and more Lutheran pastors are taking their

Doctor of Ministry degrees in spiritual direction rather than in pastoral counseling, and this trend is likely to continue.

The final "priestly function" we have enquired about has to do with the exercise of pastoral discipline within the parish. With only one and a half hours weekly given to such, there is reason to believe that the "re-Catholicization" of the Lutheran community has not yet reached deeply into the spiritual psyche. Better than seven in ten (72%) of the parish and nearly seven in ten (66%) of the clergy give pastoral discipline a low valuation of importance. That more or less three in ten of both parish and clergy give it a high rating is interesting, but does not yet suggest a convincing trend to "enforce canon law." The problem, of course, is the old Protestant problem (as discussed in the Methodist section above), viz., in a tradition of *sola Scriptura,* who is to say what is and is not right, can and cannot be done, should and should not be said, thought, believed? The exercise of ecclesiastical authority and church discipline within the Protestant world view and ethos is almost a contradictory concept. For Lutherans, who in many other categories are moving more towards serious dialogue with Rome, this matter of authority and discipline will have to be faced more substantively than has yet been the case. Rome has the Magisterium and the New Catechism but the Lutheran church does not, and how to deal with matters of authority and discipline without a set of rules tried and proven by history constitutes a major challenge today, even more so than possibly in the past, owing to the fact that in light of "form criticism" and the new biblical studies, the notion of *sola Scriptura* wears thin rather quickly.

PASTORAL FUNCTIONS

The final third of the data gathered for this study deals with five categories of what we have chosen to characterize as "pastoral functions." They are (1) pastoral counseling, (2) involvement in the social life of the parish, (3) involvement in the social life of the outside community, (4) addressing the social, moral, and political issues of the day, and (5) serving the administration of the denomination. Quite clearly there are many other activities which would easily fall into this category. Many of the respondents were kind in offering what became an almost unmanageable roster of such activities. In fact, a simple exercise in any study group of clergy looking at ministry would be to have them list as many different activities as possible in each of the three major categories being considered in this study, i.e., scholar, priest, and pastor. The management of such a group would itself constitute a major challenge to any pedagogue. But, we all must chose and select and settle for less than perfection and so we have here chosen these five activities. Though we may not find out things of interest about those other activities on that lengthy and still-growing list, we will learn some things about these five activities, and for that we think our time is being well spent.

The average Lutheran pastor spends about three and a quarter hours weekly engaged in pastoral counseling. Though some critical comments about pastoral counseling have been said already, we must never lose sight of the fact that many clergy find that counseling is what they do best and what they have most to offer within the parish setting. This elevation of traditional pastoral care, which arguably dates from the first century communities of faith, to that of a professional classification and its accompanying nomenclature of professionalism, i.e., counseling and all psychological terminology, has often resulted in individuals seeking ordination in order that they might "practice" the profession of counseling without particularly sensing a call to the ordained ministry. This has become a national phenomenon across denominational lines in this country particularly, and the problems resulting from this misuse of ministry are yet to be addressed.

In the Lutheran tradition, there seems to be some question as to the nature and significance of this particular function of ministry. That is to say, half (50%) of the laity and half (48%) of the clergy give a high importance rating to pastoral counseling, whereas, obviously, the other half of both groupings do not. By our established criteria, there is a passive satisfaction in this relationship since no position of conflict results between pastor and parish. However, there is obviously some question as to what it might mean that half of the parishes and half of the clergy come down on different sides of the "importance" question regarding pastoral counseling. Further work must be done in this category on the part of the clergy to educate the parish, but also on the part of the parish to determine to just what extent they value pastoral counseling as a meaningful and significant activity for ministry. Since more clock time is being spent on this one activity than on any other of the fifteen activities being studied here (with the exception only of functioning as an intellectual, a spiritual director, and in administration), some reasonable sense of what is being asked for and implied when the parishes and the clergy are evenly divided between whether pastoral counseling is an important function of ministry or not must be addressed.

We now come to only our second stress-inducing situation identified in this study of the Lutherans, namely, to what extent the pastor should be actively involved in the social life of the parish. Three hours are spent in this activity and nearly half (48%) of the parish believes it should bear a high valuation. However, less than one in four (24%) of the clergy feel that way and, in fact, as many of the clergy (48%) feel it should be rated low as parishioners feel it should be rated "high." Whereas nearly half of the parish feel social activities should occupy the pastor's time, less than one in four think not. The numbers are exactly reversed with the clergy, thus, a ready-made situation for stress. When the parish wants the pastor's social involvement in the faith-community and the pastor thinks less of such time, then conflict is inevitable.

Interestingly enough, the reverse pattern characterizes the question of the pastor's involvement in the social activities of the outside community. Spending only two and three-quarter hours functioning in this capacity, the pastor is faced with nearly seven in ten (68%) of the congregation who place a low valuation on this ministry, with less than one in ten (8%) of the congregation highly approving of such. Lutheran pastors are either mixed or indifferent about the meaning and nature of this aspect of ministry, with one in four (26%) evaluating this activity low and three in ten (36%) marking it "high." Mixed and confusing signals are being sent to the parish and to the community when such attitudes exist in the parish regarding the pastor's social involvements inside and outside the congregation. Naturally, these conflicting attitudes inevitably play a role in the congregation's evaluation of their pastor's effectiveness and, likewise, such conflicting perceptions will inevitably play a major role in the pastor's own self-understanding regarding obligations and responsibilities inside and outside the parish.

This tendency on the part of Lutheran parishes to be less inclined about involvement in the social life of the outside community, choosing rather to have their own parish needs seen after by the pastor, is carried over in the matter of the pastor being called upon to address the social, moral, and political issues of the day which are confronting parish and community alike. Just as in the general question of the pastor's involvement in the social life of the outside community, only 4% of the parish give a high valuation to the pastor's addressing of the issues of the day, with an astounding eight in ten (80%) giving a decidedly low rating to such activity. On the other hand, and therefore producing a stress situation, one out of four (26%) of the pastors feel that this activity should be rated high, but again, nearly half (48%) feel inclined to rate it "low." Therefore, one-quarter of the Lutheran clergy are out of step with half of the clergy and 80% of the parishioners on this point.

The message is clear, it seems, namely, Lutheran parishes generally prefer their pastors to stick to preaching and leading public worship and quite clearly to stay out of community involvements either as social activities or addressing social, moral, or political issues of the day. This close circumscription of the pastor's role *vis-a'-vis* the town or city within which the community of faith lives is cause for concern. This attitude seems to be rather disturbing and singularly devoid of what, historically, the minister's role in the community and the world has been thought to be. Certainly this has been true of Catholic priests, and to a significant degree the Anglican clergy of England. Involvement in and, indeed, full participation and leadership in the village or town in which the pastor serves, has historically been a major definition of the pastor's role as pastor. No one would seriously argue that this was not also true of the Lutheran pastors of Germany in an earlier day and even, one would argue, without benefit of data ready-to-hand, today. What must a congregation of people be thinking the role of their pastor to be when they quite clearly send a message that the pastor is essentially to "stay out of the town's social, moral, and political life" and stick to serving the rather clearly circumscribed needs of their own congregation?

Finally, we come to realize that the Lutheran pastor spends more time serving the administrative needs of the parish and denomination than in any other category of activity investigated in this study except sermon preparation. A sizeable five and one-half hours a week is given over to this task. No other activity, except the homily, whether scholarly, priestly, or pastoral, comes close to claiming this block of time. And yet, half (50%) of the parish and one in three (36%) of the clergy think this kind of activity should be valuated low on the importance scale. It would appear that the one in three parishioners (28%) and clergy (30%) who give this administrative work a high mark are having their way in view of the amount of clock time the activity is receiving. And, satisfaction seems to reign throughout the clergy and laity on this point.

It should be pointed out before we move on, that of the three major categories of activities -- scholar, priest, pastor -- it is in the "pastoral function" that three of the four stress-inducing situations exist within the Lutheran tradition. Three of five stress-generating situations in the pastoral category are differences of opinion between and among clergy and the parish over (1) the issue of involvement in the social life of the parish, (2) involvement in the social life of the outside community, and, (3) matters related to speaking out on the social, moral, and political issues of the day. Interesting it is that even though 90% of the Lutheran clergy think of themselves fundamentally as "pastors" rather than as priests or scholars, seventy-five percent of their stress is being generated in just this particular aspect of their ministry. Satisfaction is extremely high in all priestly functions and very high in scholarly functions, excepting disputes over the study of Scripture.

THE WORK WEEK

The average Lutheran pastor spends 48 hours a week in discharging ministry responsibilities, of which 19 hours (40%) of the time is allocated to "scholarly functions," 12.75 hours (26%) spent on "priestly functions," and 6.25 hours (34%) on "pastoral functions." Odd it is, but we fear typical of the clergy generally, that they spend the least amount of time doing the things they think the most important and the most amount of time doing the things they think the least important. Until this trend and pattern can somehow be reversed, the profession is destined to maintain an unacceptable level of stress-generating situations.

STRESS-INDUCERS

Let us revisit one last time the four stress areas identified in our study of the Lutheran clergy. It should be noted initially that we have found it quite remarkable that out of the fifteen activity areas only four are actually stress-inducing, whereas in the study of the Methodist clergy, we found nearly twice that many. The four have been discussed already in some detail. They are (1) conflict between the parish and the pastor over the assessed value placed upon the regular systematic study of Scripture, (2) differences of opinion over the pastor's involvement in the social life of the parish, (3) differences in expectations regarding the pastor's involvement in the social life of the outside community, and (4) questions regarding the matter of the pastor addressing the social, moral, and political issues of the day. One is struck quite readily by the surprising issue of Scripture study valuation of the Lutheran parish but not of the Lutheran pastor. That Lutheran pastors study and think they should study Scripture regularly, systematically, and exegetically is almost a truism, at least in the mind of this researcher, but that the Lutheran parish would value so little such time is rather amazing and seems to defy a simple explanation.

The other three stress-inducing situations become understandable and clearer once it is realized that Lutheran parishes, based on insights gained by this study, at least, are much more introverted on matters related to their own faith-community's spiritual well-being and very decidedly not extroverted towards the general moral and spiritual needs of the outside community in which they live and work and worship. To come to the realization that *inside the faith* the pastor must serve but *outside the faith,* maybe not, is an insight into the nature of the Lutheran experience which calls for further study. Let it suffice to say here in closing on this point, that even though we have indicated key points above at which the Lutheran church seems to be "tending towards Rome" in matters of self-definition as, for example, in their increased emphasis upon sacramentalism, the current tendency to be introverted upon faith-community life and not involved in outside community affairs separates quite clearly the Lutheran faith-community from the Catholic faith-community. We shall see shortly, involvement in the outside world is of major importance in the realization of the evangelical mission the Catholic church emphasizes and articulates in this postconciliar time and in the New Catechism.

Solutions of the four trouble areas are not readily emerging. The first stress-inducer in the "scholarly functions" category is the most readily addressed by the pastors of the Lutheran Church, who must systematically and clearly emphasize the relevance of Scripture study in the preparation of the Sunday homily and also in the personal devotional life of every parishioner. The other three -- all of which hang somewhat together under the rather unfortunate banner of "us-not- them" – require more sound teaching on the responsibility of the faith community in reaching out and serving the wider community. The teachings of the church on matters of morality and politics and a demonstration of concern for secular society by engaging the social problems of the physical and human environment in which the faith community finds itself worshiping must be emphasized.

SATISFACTION-INDUCERS

If the Lutheran community comes in for a severe scolding regarding its introversion, it certainly does not when it comes to having created a pervasive sense of satisfaction within its own clergy in the exercise of ministry. Eleven of the fifteen activity areas receive either a passive or aggressive satisfaction rating in this study, employing time allocation factors and high/low valuations by the clergy and by the parish. Heading the list of satisfaction areas we have found four of the five activities in the "scholarly functions" area. They include sermon preparation, less interest in the study of contemporary theology, serving as a spokesperson for the church's teachings, and functioning as an intellectual. We found in the "priestly functions" all of the activities receiving satisfaction marks, including the leading of public worship, presiding at the Eucharist, exercising sacramental ministries, serving as spiritual director, and exercising ecclesiastical discipline. In the "pastoral functions" category (that most preferred by the Lutheran clergy), there are two of the five which are satisfaction-inducers, viz., involvement in pastoral counseling and serving in administration of the denomination.

CATHOLIC

A brief word is in order about nomenclature by way of reiterating a point made in the opening pages of this book, namely, we will throughout this discussion use the word "Catholic" to mean the Roman Catholic church and Her tradition. In instances when we employ the word "catholic" to speak more generally of the church Universal or characteristics commonly ascribed to the church, we will only use the lower-case of the word. Otherwise, we mean solely the Roman Catholic church, Her clergy and Her tradition. When reference needs to be made to the Roman Catholic church in this section, we will simply refer to the "church."

BIOGRAPHICAL DATA (Age/Gender/Ethnicity/Academic Training)

The average priest's age in this survey is fifty-six years and, of course, there are only men in the ordained priesthood of the Roman Catholic church. An entirely different but certainly equally interesting study would be the application of many variables covered in this research instrument to women religious, i.e., nuns, of the church. That is another matter which must not detain us here. Of the respondents, 6% were minority and 58% held an advanced degree, 24% of which were doctorates.

SELF-IMAGE IN MINISTRY

Whereas in the Methodist and Lutheran traditions there has historically been the avoidance of the use of the term "priest," and, for example, with the Anglicans there is a mixed history of love-hate relationship to its use, in the Catholic church it has been the term of preference for centuries. And among Catholics, it conveys a certain perception and expectation of the clergy which will become more evident as this discussion proceeds. Better than eight in ten (82%) of the Catholic clergy prefer the term "priest" to either "scholar" (6%) or "pastor" (12%). It might be pointed out here, however, that in the Catholic church, the senior member of the clerical staff of a parish is customarily referred to by official title as "Pastor," so that the use of the term "pastor" conveys a slightly different self-image and parish role than is necessarily implied in the Protestant traditions where "pastor" may simply mean an ordained minister. As mentioned in the opening pages of this book, we anticipated finding the four traditions — Lutheran, Catholic, Methodist, Episcopal — preferring, in order, of listing the titles "Scholar," "Priest," and "Pastor." However, we have been foiled in this expectation since both Lutherans and Methodists seem much more to prefer the term "pastor" to either of the other two. It was a domain assumption that the Lutheran clergy would prefer to think of themselves as "scholars." But with the Catholic clergy, we have not been disappointed in their anticipated selection of the self-descriptive term of "priest" rather than scholar or pastor.

By way of reminder, the reader is to understand that what is being sought in this study is the identification of "stress" and "satisfaction" areas of ministry within the four traditions —Methodist, Lutheran, Catholic and Episcopalians. We have determined that we will divide some fifteen areas of ministry activity into the easily distinguishable classifications of scholar, priest, and pastor, each classification being ascribed five distinct activity areas.

The determination as to whether there is stress or satisfaction in any particular activity is based on the assessment of the data analysis such that in addition to noting the amount of actual clock time the clergy spend discharging a particular activity (called Time Task Allocation or TTA), we also look at the clergy's perception of the parish's attitude about each of these activities (called Parish Task Value Assessment or PTVA), as well as the clergy's own attitude about these specific activities (called Clergy Task Value Assessment or CTVA). We rank the response on the basis of percentages, indicating a mark of high importance (60% and up) or of low importance (40% or less), with a general disregard for the middle range of 40%-60%, presuming the indifference to be of no consequence in the analysis. Stress, then, is presumed present when there is a divergence of valuation between the parish and the pastor and satisfaction when there is general balance in valuation, whether that valuation is high or "low."

If both the clergy and the parish think a particular activity, say studying Scripture, is of high value, then no stress occurs, but rather general satisfaction. If, on the other hand, the parish values an activity highly while the clergy place a low estimation on its importance, then we have determined that a stress-inducing conflict has arisen or is potentially present. Therefore, the lower the number of instances of stress-inducing situations we identify among the clergy and the greater the number of satisfaction-inducing situations, the higher the level of overall satisfaction with the pastoral situation in which we believe the clergy and parish find themselves.

SCHOLARLY FUNCTIONS

Five specific activities have been classified in this category and they are (1) sermon preparation, (2) studying theology, (3) studying Scripture, (4) serving as a spokesperson for the teachings of the church, and (5) functioning as an intellectual. It is presumed that if a clergy person thinks of himself (in all references to the clergy in this section we will use the masculine pronoun given the fact that no women are Catholic clergy) as a "scholar" in any traditional sense, surely that self-image will manifest itself in at least these five activities.

In the area of sermon preparation, Catholic clergy spend four and a half hours per week preparing the Sunday homily. Eight in ten of the parish and nine in ten of the clergy give a high mark to the importance of this activity. Satisfaction, then, is the character of the clergy/parish relationship when it comes to a mutual agreement as to the great importance of the sermon and its preparation. It has not been too long ago that the Catholic clergy came under general criticism from the Protestant world over their lack of attention to the "proclamation of the Word," with the exception of the preaching orders of the church. That can no longer be said, whether it was ever justified or not. Catholic seminaries today are placing a major emphasis upon the value of the homiletic ministry and the need for well-developed skills and habits in the preparation of sermons.

The accusation in the past has been that Catholic priests spend little time on the sermon and concentrate primarily upon the liturgical functions of presiding at the Mass. Protestants, it should be pointed out, too often under-value the centrality of the Eucharist in the life of the Catholic community and, therefore, when the priest and the congregation spend a disproportionate amount of worship time celebrating Eucharist rather than preaching, the implications are that the sermon is insignificant in the face of Holy Communion. Catholics would never think of the relationship of the sermon to the Eucharist as separate or subject to ranking as to importance. The Mass is central to the life of the church and the sermon is part of the total liturgical experience of celebrating Eucharist. More on this point will be said later in this discussion. Suffice it to say here that the Catholic parish and priest alike agree and are satisfied with the time spent in sermon preparation.

However, the same cannot be said about the study time clergy give to theology and contemporary theologians, for while the priest spends two and a half hours weekly studying theology and better than three in ten of them (34%) think this is of high value, just over one in ten (12%) of the parish so value theological study. In fact, better than seven in ten (72%) members of the parish actually give a low mark of importance to such study, while only 16% of the clergy think it unimportant. The majority of the priests, however, have chosen not to give either a high or low valuation to such study (50%). Nevertheless, stress is induced when one compares the one in three clergy saying high to seven in ten parishioners saying low to the study of theology. This, as we have suggested in our earlier discussions of the Methodist and Lutheran clergy, is an indication of a lack of appreciation on the part of members of the faith community of the need and significance in the ongoing intellectual life and further development of the clergy's own understanding of the church and Her teachings to continue to stay up and stay sharp in theological matters. One would be totally astounded to learn, for instance, that individuals think it a waste of time for their physician or their attorney to take time to continue to study the latest writings and developments in medicine and the law. How is it, then, that parishioners think nothing of valuing only slightly the study of theology by their pastors and priests? Is it possible that the medical and legal communities have done a better job of educating their constituencies on the importance of the professionals' ongoing development and enrichment than has the church and Her clergy? This should be a major point of concern on the part of the bishops of the church in their pastoral leadership of the diocese, for if members of the faith community think little of their pastors continuing to keep up with theological discussion then how can members of the parish expect to continue to deepen in their own understanding and experience of the faith as taught by the church?

And not only in theological study, but even in the study of Scripture we find such an attitude. The priest spends two and three-quarter hours weekly in the systematic study of Scripture with nearly half (48%) of the clergy giving this activity a high mark, while less than one in three (28%) of the parish so value time spent in the study of Scripture by the pastor. More of the parish (30%) actually rate this activity low on its value scale! In the postconciliar church and under the mandate from the leadership of Vatican II, the church has put forth a concerted effort to emphasize the study of scripture among the laity as well as among the clergy and religious. Indeed, a great deal of work and effort has gone, and continues to go, into the development of study helps and resources for those interested in Scripture studies. Never before has the church found Herself on the initiative in encouraging, admonishing, and providing a myriad of opportunities for the systematic and scholarly study of Scripture at all levels of learning, from the nursery to the pastor's study, than is in evidence today. Is it possible that the church has failed in Her mission to heighten awareness of the centrality of Scripture study in Her life? While the Scripture must always be interpreted in light of the teachings of the Magisterium, acquaintance with the Scripture has never before been so emphasized as it has since the opening sessions of the Second Vatican Council. If ever there was a clear message to bishops and clergy alike in terms of an area of further need for teaching and instruction, it is here — namely, the laity must be admonished to value the study of Scripture as well as theology by the clergy if they, themselves, are to be the beneficiaries of deepening understanding of the faith. The danger to the health of the church today is the possibility that the average member of the parish sitting in the pew on Sunday is quite happy for their pastors not to be involved in continuing to deepen their intellectual under- standing of the faith and in turn quite happy not to be bothered with such study themselves. Other implications and explanations will be explored later, but certainly this is a stress-inducing situation for clergy when they find little support from the congregation in the time they feel they need to spend in the study of Scripture.

More encouraging by far is the next set of statistics. Priests spend an average of four hours a week serving in the role as spokesperson for the teachings of the church. And, by way of fostering satisfaction with this priority ministry, just over half (54%) of the parish and almost half (46%) of the clergy think this activity highly important, with less than two in ten (18%) of the parish and less than two in ten (16%) of the clergy giving it a decidedly low mark of importance. The authoritative teachings of the church need a spokesperson inside the parish and outside in the world and it is the priest who discharges that responsibility, and that with encouragement and support from the parish and fellow clergy alike. With the exception of the preparation of the Sunday sermon, there are no categories of activity within the scholarly function of ministry in which the priest finds himself more affirmed and encouraged by clergy and parish alike, than in serving as an authoritative spokesperson for the teachings of the church. This is, indeed, a positive note of satisfaction for church and clergy alike.

The final area of activity in the scholarly functions of ministry exercised by priests is that of functioning as a valued and respected intellectual within the life of the parish. He spends nearly five hours a week (4.75) serving in this capacity and, again, as with the role as spokesperson, there is reason to find satisfaction in this function. Nearly half of the clergy (46%) and better than three in ten (32%) of the parish give this activity a high mark. And, though four in ten (40%) of the parish and 28% of the clergy give it a low mark of importance, the ratio of high to low is sufficiently balanced as to not, according to our formula for analysis discussed in Chapter Two, be the source of stress for the clergy. At most one could say that a better job might be done by the clergy to emphasize to their own congregations the significance of the pastor being intellectually informed and astute in matters related both to parish life and to the life of the community at large. Historically, certainly, the parish priest functioned as a leading, if not the leading, intellectual of the community as well as the parish. One need only think of Ireland and her glorious history to be reminded that the village priest was not merely the pastor of a local congregation but was a person of note for the entire community. Today, it is the unusual priest or pastor who has taken the time to reach a level of formal education such that he is respected by the parish and the community at large as an intellectual. A case could be made that his time is better spent discharging his duties as a priest of the sacraments rather than as a dispenser of intellectual insights with the local *intelligentsia*. Yet an equally convincing case can be made that the clergy today, Catholic and Protestant alike, have given far too much ground to the secular world by failing to continue to grow intellectually in the ways of the world such that their presence would be valued and respected in discussions of affairs of state and community for the well-being of all members of society. A pastor need not be a dunce in worldly knowledge just because he is astute as a liturgist, and to allow oneself to be smothered in parish functions at the expense of developing intellectually is a misplaced allocation of time, for time spent witnessing in the world to the intellectual life of the church is time well spent.

PRIESTLY FUNCTIONS

The five activities we have chosen to characterize as "priestly" are (1) leading public worship, (2) presiding at Eucharist, (3) exercising other sacramental ministries, (4) spiritual direction, and (5) discipline in the parish. As with any list, it is too short or too restrictive or too one-sided or too parochial, yet, one must begin and end somewhere. After careful consideration and in the formation of the research instrument, i.e., the survey, these five finally won out and so we will stick with them for good or ill. It must be pointed out here, even if it means giving away the punch of this category, that the levels of satisfaction in all five areas of activity are extremely high. Indeed, the levels of concurrence between priest and parish in three of the five activities is above eight in ten and even where there is a general agreement that an activity is valued low, the concurrence is at six in ten. One is led to observe even at the outset that the mutuality of respect and alignment between the priest and parish in these "priestly functions" are great grounds for optimism and hope in terms of the church's future relationship with its ministering clergy. Satisfaction reigns supreme throughout the categories of priestly function, precisely that category of function to which the Catholic clergy from the beginning have chosen as their domain, namely, that of "priest." At the risk of being self-congratulatory, this author is pleased to have rather nicely identified and circumscribed for closer analysis these five activities precisely because there is such universal agreement between priest and parish as to their importance and their overall evaluation.

In separating out "leading the congregation in public worship" from "presiding over the Eucharist," we were anxious to know just how priests assessed these liturgical events. Though the majority of liturgical functions center around the Eucharistic Celebration, there are sufficient numbers of liturgical events other than Eucharist to merit this separation. And, to our delight, we find that better than nine in ten parishioners (94%) and nine in ten priests (96%) placed a high mark on the importance of these events. In spending better than eight hours in a week (8.25) engaged in leading non-Eucharistic liturgical functions, and with these extremely high levels of approval mandated by both parish and clergy, the priest is well-advised to continue seeking out opportunities for such activity. Only in the Eucharistic celebrations do we find the priest spending this much time on any of the fifteen activities being analyzed in this study.

Satisfaction, to be sure, is extremely high here and it may suggest to us that the parish is much more interested in "public worship" and liturgical activities than they are in knowing about, or being concerned with, how much time the priest spends studying Scripture and theology in preparation for a sermon.

Throughout this entire study of thousands of clergy and gathered bits of data, we have found no activity, excepting the Catholic priest presiding at the Eucharist, which has received a one hundred percent acclamation of high value by both parish and pastor. Spending eight and one-quarter hours a week celebrating Eucharist with a 100% approval rating by parish and priests alike seems obviously where priests should concentrate their time and energy. The postconciliar movement can be rightly and justifiably proud of these statistics, for it was the intention of the church from the outset of Vatican II to reaffirm the centrality of the Eucharist in the life of the Catholic church. Obviously the church has succeeded in this effort. That the life and faith of the church centers around the Eucharist and takes its energy and comfort from this celebration has been the teaching of the church from Apostolic times. Today we see the church, Her clergy and Her entire family, embracing this position at the parish level in an undisputed show of unity.

Close behind the Eucharistic celebration in terms of parish and priestly affirmations of value is the exercising of sacramental functions of ministry such as hearing confessions, baptizing, absolutions, anointing the sick, etc. The priest is spending four and a half hours weekly in such activity, and better than eight in ten (84%) members of the parish and better than eight in ten (84%) of the clergy think these activities should be ranked "high." Again, the level of satisfaction among the clergy and congregation is outstanding and such time spent is obviously greatly valued and assessed highly. When all else fails in the parish situation where the priest is floundering for a sense of mission and duty to the congregation, the priest would do no better than to take a hint from this study and "do something liturgical" to bring the parish around to a healthy level of contentment. More study of Scripture and theology and, as we will see later in this section, more involvement in the social, moral, and political issues of the day will not do it. Indeed, such activity may alienate the parish even further. However, with virtually everyone, parish and priest alike, indicating a really high approval rating of public worship and "sacramental" ministry activities, why not go with these types of activities? Surely one can exercise the teaching mission of the church through liturgical events, and if one is justifiably intent upon deeper study in theology and Scripture, and one feels morally obliged to address the moral and political issues of the day, then do so within the framework of these highly approved liturgical events in the life of the parish. The parish, therefore, is continually being affirmed in its love of worship and the priest is discharging his duty as a teacher and moral leader. Everyone wins, and no one seems to lose.

Thanks both to a real sense of urgency about spiritual formation among the laity and to a bold affirmation of the centrality of spiritual direction in the life of the parish initiated by the Second Vatican Council, parish priests are spending more than three hours a week (3.25) engaged in spiritual direction with a better than four in ten (42%) approval rating by the parish and better than a six in ten (64%) by the clergy. Only slightly better than one in ten (16%) of the parish and only one in ten (10%) of the clergy give the ministry of spiritual direction a low mark. The pursuit of formal training and education, both in theory and practice, in the field of spiritual direction among both the laity and the clergy, has not enjoyed such support in the life of the church in any time this century to the degree that it is now. It might be argued that the church has never seen the laity as enthusiastic about spirituality generally, and spiritual direction and matters of formation specifically, as is currently occurring. Certification programs, degree programs, sabbatical leave programs, and short-term easy-to-access programs for clergy, religious, and laity alike have sprung up all over the country and, judging from the church papers, has yet to reach a saturation point. The Graduate Theological Foundation of Indiana has even launched its P.R.I.M.E. Program (Partnering Resources in Ministry Education) in which it partners with diocesan sponsored certification programs and provides a degree-completion opportunity for clergy and laity alike who wish to pursue their interest in spiritual direction to the Master of Theology or the Doctor of Ministry level. Never have the Catholic diocese and Archdiocese of this country seen such a rush to subscribe to any and all educational opportunities providing training and instruction in spirituality than they are presently enjoying.

If the exercise of ecclesiastical discipline is very much not desired or approved among the Lutherans and Methodists, the same can certainly be said of the Catholic church today as well. Spending two and a half hours a week in the exercise of discipline according to the canons of the church including, of course, its corollary in counseling, the priest finds that fewer than one in ten (9%) of the parish and fewer than two in ten (18%) of the clergy give such activity a high mark of approval. Rather, nearly seven in ten (66%) of the laity and almost as many (59%) of the clergy give it a decidedly low mark. Stress-induction seems not to occur due to the mutuality of feeling generally between the laity and the clergy on this point. If either group felt strongly the other way, then stress would obviously occur. What wasn't measured here, but would certainly merit a follow-up study, is the feeling of the bishops of the diocese regarding such matters. Contrary to general suspicions among many Protestants regarding the meaning and nature of Catholic discipline, parish priests are actually spending very little time disciplining their parishioners and that with the general approval of the parish and their colleagues. In the Catholic Church, where discipline of a formal sort is possible, owing to the reality of the authority structure of the church embodied in the Magisterium and explained to the laity in the recently released and magnificently done *New Catechism of the Catholic Church*, priests exercise such discipline to a knowing constituency within the context of pastoral counseling and spiritual direction. In other words, the priest doesn't merely bind and strap the errant parishioner, but rather, instructs and guides the recipient of discipline within the framework of prayer and penance. It is all done under the careful and nurturing hand of the church through the office of the bishop and within the structures of the church's canons. Discipline, then, in the Catholic Church, is a mechanism for pastoral care and spiritual instruction rather than a means of pugilistic sadism as too often portrayed from the outside. Mutuality of satisfaction between parish and priest characterizes this essential component of priestly function in the Catholic church.

PASTORAL FUNCTIONS

The five areas of activities classified as "pastoral" in nature are (1) pastoral counseling, (2) involvement in the social life of the parish, (3) involvement in the social life of the wider community, (4) publicly addressing social, moral, and political issues of the day, and (5) serving the administration needs of the parish and diocese. Many more activities should be included here but time and management of the survey precluded expanding this rather wide field of pastoral functions. These five, however, few will argue against. Our findings bear out our initial expectation that these five activities reflect a general attitude and perception about the nature of ministry across the board — laity and clergy, Catholic and Protestant alike.

The typical Catholic priest spends over three hours a week (3.25) involved in individual and family pastoral counseling. Four in ten (42%) of the parish and four in ten (40%) of the clergy believe this pastoral function should be rated high on the list of priorities for parish ministry. Only about two in ten parishioners (22%) and priests (18%) felt it should receive a low mark. Historically, pastoral counseling was the fundamental domain of the parish priest, but in earlier days it was thought of as pastoral care and was devoid of the professional trappings attendant upon the term "pastoral counseling" today. Now, we have professional organizations of variously credentialed and trained clergy and laity skilled in the particulars of psychological services and compliant with the increasing litany of government rules applicable to the practice of such counseling in the parish setting. It can be argued that many in the parish now intentionally seek out spiritual direction rather than pastoral counseling to meet their personal needs. To the extent that the clergy of a parish or diocese, and of the church generally, have done a good job in teaching the laity about the nature and scope as well as the limitations of each of these ministry services, pastoral counseling and spiritual direction, to that extent, and to that extent only, the laity are able to make an informed decision about the type of ministry they seek out from their clergy. It can be argued that old-fashioned "pastoral care" can be found somewhere between spiritual direction and pastoral counseling, but much more work needs to be done in this area of educating the parish as to the significance and meaning of the difference. There is, certainly, room here for a data base study of parishioners' perceptions and attitudes about the distinctions.

Half (50%) of the parish believes the priest should be actively involved in the social life of the parish and nearly four in ten (38%) of the clergy feel likewise. Spending three and a half hours a week in such activity, priests, however, more than twice as frequently give this kind of ministry a low mark of importance (32% clergy versus 14% laity). The fact that 36% of the laity are indifferent about this ministry is one of the reasons we indicate an acceptable level of satisfaction all the way around with this activity. As the number of priests continue to decline and many of their non-sacramental ministry activities are taken over by the laity, there will necessarily need to be both an adjustment by the parish and significant teaching to the parish as to the availability of the priest for such social life involvement. When every parish had priests to spare, their presence at every social event in the life of the parish was taken for granted. Today, it is the rare occasion in which a typical parish priest has the time and can justify the effort to be involved in mere social events. Only time will tell how Catholic parishes make the adjustment from "high visibility," of the clergy to extremely "low visibility" but adjustments there will need to be. Significant study of this anticipated major shift in the ambiance of the Catholic parish is crying out to be done.

Numbers are much different, though the time spent is about the same (3.5 hours), when it comes to priestly involvement in the social life of the wider community. Whereas five in ten of the laity highly valued the priest's involvement in the social life of the parish, just over one in ten (12%) of the laity give a high mark to his involvement in the wider community, with nearly six in ten of the laity (56%) giving such ministry a decidedly 'low" ranking. Likewise, and thus satisfaction-inducing, the clergy only at two in ten (20%) give it high rank, whereas nearly half (48%) give it a "low' reading on the valuation scale. At least the parish and priest are agreed that time spent on social activities in the wider community is more or less a waste of the pastor's time. No stress here, rather, a genuine awareness of the realities of limitation on the pastor's time. The priest might better do other things such as lead worship or work on the sermon than get involved in community social life.

Stress, however, occurs when the issue of addressing social, moral, and political topics within the wider community arises. Spending two and a half hours a week in such ministry, less than two in ten (16%) of the parish but four in ten (40%) of the clergy give this high marks, with over half the parish (52%) and over four in ten (42%) of the clergy giving it a low ranking. Stress is generated here, both between the parish and the pastor (40% of the pastors saying high and 52% of the parish saying low), as well as between and among clergy who are almost equally divided between the approval and disapproval ratings (40% high to 52% low). Obviously, what is at work here is a fundamental challenge to the definition of ministry as embodied by the Catholic priest. Is he, or is he not, to be actively involved in a public manner with the issues of the day affecting morality and political life? This is a question that cries out for an answer.

58   John H. Morgan

Since the Second Vatican Council, there is a growing sense that within the teaching office of the church there needs to be further work done on a "theology of the priesthood," especially in light of today's rapid and radical decline in their numbers. To what extent they are to be reduced, for lack of a better term, to solely (I do not say merely) sacerdotal or sacramental forms of ministry, is to be decided within the framework of the numbers of priests available, numbers of parishes in need of priests, and the amount of time on the clock for the discharge of priestly duties. Few informed theologians and church leaders will argue with the suggestion that this particular problem will constitute a major item on the agenda of the 21st Century Church.

It would appear that sheer numbers (numbers of priests and numbers of parishes) will be a major factor in setting the theological agenda for the next century, for no matter how nicely the theological formulation of the church's teaching on the meaning and nature of the priesthood will prove to be, the point is muted radically in the face of a growing imbalance of priests to parishes. This numerical fact itself renders much high-flung speculative theologizing about the nature of the priesthood moot if not comical. I am reminded of a story of a store owner when asked by a customer about the price of a particular item, and in response to the price quoted the customer says, "But I could get it down the street for less." To the store owner's query as to why the customer didn't make the purchase down the street, the customer responded, "They were temporarily out of the item." "Oh," responds the store owner, "if I were out of the item, I would let you have it free." The niceties of a theology of the priesthood will inevitably fall meaningless on the deaf ears of the underserved laity in the face of a declining, if not disappearing, priesthood!

Finally and happily, there is general satisfaction among the clergy and laity about the six and one-half hours a week the priest spends serving the administrative needs of the parish and diocese. Three in ten laity and clergy give this activity a high mark, while better than three in ten (34%) of the laity and nearly half (48%) of the clergy give it a low ranking. The balance, however, is sufficiently close as to avoid stress. What is missing is a deep appreciation and understanding of the need for, and value of, this time in administration being given by the priest to the church. Again, we are forced to muse about the future and wonder whether priests in the 21st Century Church will be altogether exempted from such "deaconal" ministries of management and administration when they are fundamentally responsible for the exercise of the sacramental ministry of the church. A well-established and viable core of deacons will certainly cause the parish and the priests of the church to reevaluate the reasonableness of the priest spending six and a half hours a week in administering parish and diocesan affairs. A data base study addressing this issue would be of great service to the church as we attempt to sort out what the 21st century is likely to look like in view of the shifting numbers within the ranks of the clergy. Ironic or prophetic it is that while the church is growing numerically by leaps and bounds among the laity, the numbers of clergy and religious continue to decline exponentially fast.

If satisfaction in ministry with little attendant stress is what we have sought and what we would all mutually agree to be an ideal situation, then we have come closest to it in the Catholic Church, with only three of the fifteen activity areas generating any stress and twelve of the fifteen generating satisfaction among clergy and laity alike. Only in two groups of activities — study of theology and Scripture and involvement in issues of the day — do we find stress and that mostly between a difference of opinion as to how the priest should spend his time. In the three categories of ministry function — scholarly, priestly, pastorally — we find the two study activities in the scholarly function, the moral and political issues in the pastoral function, and the priestly function completely clear of any identified stress-inducing situations. How thoroughly pleasing this level of contentment must be for the bishops of the diocese of the church who are faced with a decline in priests' numbers and a rise in parish demands for pastoral services. Could it be that there is a correlation between a decline in the number of clergy and the realization on the part of the laity that they must not place undue demands upon the clergy and, thereby, avoid stress-inducing situations? Let us hope not, for it would be a sad commentary on religious life generally if one were to suggest that with a decline in clergy numbers, those who remain find working conditions improved! Rather, I think it fair to surmise from the data that as the laity begin to realize that the priest's time is becoming more and more limited owing to a decline in the numbers of those serving in the priesthood, the laity will pull back their demands on the priest's time and give full latitude to his own judgments about the expenditure of his limited time.

THE WORK WEEK

Not surprising, but disturbing, is the discovery that the average parish priest spends sixty-four hours a week in the exercise of his ministry, and given the fact that his average age is fifty-six years, there is cause for concern here, if not alarm. Of this sixty-four hours per week spent in ministry, the priest spends eighteen and a half hours (nearly 30%) of his time discharging "scholarly functions" such as study and sermon preparation. He also spends twenty-six and three-quarter hours engaged in "priestly functions" such as presiding at Eucharist (about 40% of his week). Finally, he spends the balance of his time (30% or better than nineteen hours) engaged in "pastoral functions." It has been argued, and within Protestant circles I have heard it frequently, that because the Catholic priest is celibate he can rightly be expected by his parish to spend a disproportionately greater amount of time in ministry than can the Protestant clergy be reasonably expected to do, since most of them (94%) are married. This argument is disarmed when one imagines the backdoor implications that Protestant clergy are "hampered" by their own families in the exercise of their ministries. The equation argument about celibacy and family life best be left alone, being sure to create more problems than it solves or merits. A more obvious insight is the realization that with declining numbers of priests and increasing numbers of Catholics (one of the nation's faster, if not fastest growing Christian bodies) there are simply greater demands on the priests' time and, thus, a fifteen hour day becomes standard operating procedure by many parish clergy. Bishops at this point must become very concerned and actively, even aggressively, engage in addressing the issue of Time Task Allocations by their clergy. Bishops will be the ones to instruct the parishes regarding the fair and proper use of priests' time. It is certainly time now to begin to instruct parishes in these matters, for when the 21st Century is upon us the problem of parish demands and priests' time will be at crisis-level proportions. If, however, parishes have been systematically and carefully trained and educated in the right and proper use of the priest's time, then the problem is resolved and may, as with the decline in vocations, become a source of continuing strength in spiritual growth and leadership among the laity. This potential vice can effectively be converted into a virtue with proper instruction and training of the laity under the pastoral nurture of the bishops of the church.

STRESS-INDUCERS

We have already identified the three stress-inducing situations common in Catholic parishes today, viz., a conflict of priorities between the priest and the parish over his use of time in the study of theology and Scripture and a conflict over the nature of his addressing the social, moral, and political issues of the day. In all three instances the priest wants to spend more time discharging these ministries — study and social issues — and the parish wants him to spend less. In all three it can reasonably be argued that the priest is right and the parish is wrong in its expectations. Therefore, it falls the responsibility of the priest to engage in corrective explanations through instruction of the parish regarding the value and meaning of theology and Scripture study for his own spiritual and intellectual growth and development. Their concomitant benefit in the form of better and more effective sermons and educational programs will also result.

Regarding social and moral issues, the pastor must effectively convey to the parish that it falls squarely within his responsibility in the teaching office of the priest to engage the wider community in a discussion of the moral and social issues confronting society at large and the parish directly. His teaching office and his position as a spokesperson for the church makes it imperative that he engage these issues publicly as a servant of the church and a representative of Christ. This, too, becomes an opportunity for the priest to nurture the parish into a deeper and more meaningful understanding and appreciation of the teachings of the church and of their own faith journey.

SATISFACTION-INDUCERS

"Satisfying" rather than "satisfied" should be the way we think of the parish-priest relationship in the Catholic church. "Satisfied" implies inert contentment, whereas "satisfying" suggests mutuality of respect between priest and parish. Neither the Catholic priest nor his parish must ever think of themselves as content, for in contentment lurks inertia and indolence, passivity and lack of vocation. The Catholic church is calling for increased effort in evangelism, in the spreading of the Gospel of Christ and the nurturing growth of His church. This mission of evangelization is greatly served by the current situation of a deeply felt sense of mutual respect between the parish and the priest. The church is in a unique situation of being able to move forward with its mission given the high level of positive affirmation which exists between priest and parish.

EPISCOPAL

BIOGRAPHICAL DATA (Age/Gender/Ethnicity/Academic Training)

The average age for the responding Episcopal clergy was 53 years of age, with 6% from women and no response from ethnic minorities within the clergy ranks. Less than one in four (22%) actually held an advanced degree beyond the ordination degree and of those who did hold a graduate degree, less than one-quarter of those were doctorates.

SELF-IMAGE IN MINISTRY

We set out with presuppositions about the Methodists, Lutherans, and Catholics when it came to identifying themselves as pastors, scholars, and priests and, as we have already noted, we were proven in error in one of these viz., the Lutheran clergy think of themselves primarily as "pastors rather than "scholars." When we came to the Episcopal clergy, there was some ambivalence on our part for within the Anglican Communion, and certainly within the church of England, the "scholarly" characteristic of the historic ministry is well established, while the High church tradition in England and abroad quite commonly employs the term "priest" to designate the clergy. It might be noted in passing that in an earlier study in the ecclesiastical sociology series, entitled *Who Becomes Bishop?: A Study of Episcopal Clergy*, it was discovered that less than 2% of the Bishops in the Episcopal church hold doctorates in theology and none are members of Phi Beta Kappa, thus leading to the further notion that among the American clergy of the Anglican tradition scholarship is not so highly valued as has historically been the case in England. English bishops have historically been theological and biblical scholars, whereas in the American church, they have distinguished themselves, with rare exception, as administrators only. So, when we came to an investigation into the self-image of the American clergy within the Anglican tradition, we were unable to anticipate self-image. By asking the question we found the answer! Just over six in ten (62%) of Episcopal clergy in the U.S. prefer the designation "priest" to describe their ministry while three in ten prefer "pastor." Only 14% of them prefer to think of themselves as "scholar," whereas 86% of them place this designation last in the list of scholar, priest, and pastor. A surprising 6% place the designation "priest" last in the list as well.

SCHOLARLY FUNCTIONS

The Episcopal clergy average far more time per week in sermon preparation than do the other three traditions, with eight and one-half hours spent on homiletical work weekly. The preaching tradition is strong in some quarters of the Anglican church including the maintenance of a College of Preachers at their cathedral in Washington, D.C. Nearly three out of four members of the parish place a high value on this time and eight in ten of the clergy do as well. Less than one in ten (8%) of the parish value this with a low importance rating and half of that percentage on the part of the clergy. At a time when the Episcopal church U.S.A. is experiencing massive shifts of self-consciousness in terms of liturgical reform and definitions of ministry, a strong point of continuity is that of the importance placed on the sermon by both clergy and laity.

Two stress-inducing areas of ministry for Episcopal clergy, as they see it, have to do with a conflict in the value of time spent in the study of theology and Scripture. We have seen this trend in other traditions discussed here as well. Better than eight in ten (82%) of the Episcopal laity think time spent studying theology of low importance in the exercise of ministry, with only 6% valuing such time as of high importance. However, among the clergy, there is a strikingly high percentage of clergy valuing theology as of low value at 50%, but with a surprising 20% (better than three times that among the laity) valuing theological study highly. The stress anticipated in this relationship comes between both the pastor and the parish (20% and 6% respectively) and within the ranks of the clergy themselves (20% high and 50% low). We will later note that only the Methodist clergy value theological study lower than Episcopalians and the Episcopal laity are by far the most critical of their pastors studying theology.

With regard to the study of Scripture, we find a similar trend among Episcopalians. Again, stress is generated over the conflict resulting from nearly half (48%) of the laity placing a low rank on such time spent, while just over half (52%) of the clergy give it a high rating. Somewhat disturbing is the 14% of the clergy who rate Scripture study as low in importance in their ministry, but equally of concern is the fact that only about one in four (28%) of the laity actually rate Scripture study "high."

If stress is being generated for the Episcopal clergy over differences of opinion regarding the amount of time they think they should spend studying theology and Scripture and their perceptions of what they think the laity expect in these matters, we find "satisfaction" being generated not only with mutual agreement about time spent on sermon preparation, but also on the role of the pastor as a spokesperson for the church and the pastor's role as a member of the intelligentsia of the parish. In both instances, the laity are quite happy for the pastor *not to function in either capacity to any great extent,* with only 24% of the laity thinking the role of spokesperson is important and 36% thinking the same of the pastor as an intellectual within the parish. The clergy seem to be in more or less agreement about these two roles, with only 26% of the clergy rating highly the role of spokesperson and 38% rating highly that of intellectual. What is interesting is the fact that the parish seems to be more or less equally divided over whether to rate high or low the pastor's role as an intellecutal (34% say "yes" and 36% say "no"). Again, that the pastor is not thought of by the parish (that is, as the pastor perceives the parish) as a spokesperson for the teachings of the church is an indication, as we found among the Methodists and Lutherans, that the Episcopal pastor is thought of by the parish as primarily responsible for ministering to the pastoral needs of the parish. The priest is neither a spokesperson to the world about the teaching of the church (an evangelical mission) nor an intellectual (contrary to the long-standing tradition within the church of England where the local parish clergy person was often the most educated member of the community). Much has already been said about the reality of the decline in importance of the clergy demonstrating intellectual prowess outside the circumscribed role of the parish's pastoral needs. Here, the Episcopal tradition confirms our findings.

PRIESTLY FUNCTIONS

There are five specific areas of ministry activity selected for this category – worship, Eucharist, sacramental ministry, spiritual direction, and discipline. Whereas we found two of the five areas of ministry activity in the Scholarly Functions category stress-ridden, we find here only one, viz., having to do with the role of clergy as spiritual director. Before we consider that activity and the problematics raised for the Episcopal clergy, let us begin with the two highest categories of satisfaction related to time-task allocations. These are (1) leading the congregation in worship, and (2) celebrating Eucharist. The

Anglican tradition is self-defined as a "sacramental" church and the emphasis upon liturgy generally and upon the Eucharist specifically is, therefore, anticipated. This has not always been true, certainly with respect to the Eucharist. In an earlier time in this country and in various places across the globe, Eucharist was not called Eucharist at all, but Holy Communion, and was not celebrated weekly or daily as is common today. Monthly celebrations by clergy not called "priest" and a liturgy not called "Eucharist" was quite common in what came to be known as "Low church" parishes. Even today, they are not unknown. However, that aside, it is clear that the Episcopal church in this country has become increasingly a self-consciously sacramental church with heavy emphasis upon worship and Eucharist. Nine out of every ten (90%) members of the laity place a high value mark on the "leading of public worship" as a good functional use of the pastor's time and the clergy beat that with 92%. When it comes to celebrating Eucharist, those percentages rise to 96% laity and 100% clergy. No member of the clergy nor the laity in this study gave the Eucharist a low mark and only 2% of each of the clergy and laity gave the leading of public worship a low mark. Quite decidedly, the Anglican communion in this country is centered upon its worship life and the greatest degree of mutual satisfaction between clergy and laity over the use of ministry time is realized here.

Stress is generated when it comes to the pastor serving as a spiritual director. Though "catholic" in its spirituality, at least up to the most recent of times in this country, the Anglican Church has, nevertheless, always maintained a strong commitment to spiritual formation among its clergy. The spirituality tradition of Anglicanism is, of course, indisputably strong in examples and long in duration. We need not, therefore, engage in a litany of spiritual thinkers within Anglicanism nor in the listing of their prestigious production in this field. (My book, *The Anglican Mind*, has substantially spoken to this topic). Where the stress seems to be generated is in the divergence of importance placed on the pastor as spiritual director, seen in the fact that less than one in four (24%) of the laity think this a high value for clergy time, whereas better than twice that number (58%) of the clergy feel it deserves a high ranking. Only 12% of the clergy give it a low ranking, as compared to nearly half (44%) of the laity. There is obviously a need and call for more education of the laity by the clergy if the clergy intend to receive a favorable affirmation from the parish in their spending time engaged in spiritual direction. Wherever there is this degree of divergence, the situation is fraught with potential stress and conflict.   The only meaningful solution to the issue is for the clergy to engage in an all-out effort to educate the parish in terms of the nature and meaning and, indeed, value of spiritual direction. *Only among the Episcopalians, surprisingly enough, do we find the issue of spiritual direction being the source of stress and conflict.*

Finally, in the area of "priestly functions," we come to that most troublesome of responsibilities traditionally assumed by the parish pastor and that is the issue of "discipline." It is an area of "satisfaction" rather than "stress" for Episcopalians, for neither the clergy (74%) nor the laity (76%) think it worthy of more than a low ranking. Only 4% of the laity and 6% of the clergy venture a high mark for this ministry function. By far, the Episcopal clergy rate this function lower than any of the other traditions – three times lower than Catholics and five times, more or less, than Methodists and Lutherans. In view of recent history within the denomination, the Episcopal church U.S.A. has had its share of conflicts nationally regarding major issues of discipline and authority. The entire national church appears sometimes to be in a state of crisis over the issue of ecclesiastical jurisdiction in matters of faith and practice. There are dioceses and regions of the country where the church has attempted to exercise extremely circumscribed disciplinary action and others where anarchy seems to be the mode of operation. Their national papers, both for the laity and for the theologically astute, seem to be overwhelmed with the whole topic of the church's jurisdiction in matters of discipline and authority.

The topics of ordination of women and liturgical reform back several years ago seem to have set the stage for an ongoing struggle for control within the leadership of the denomination. The denomination has seen the rise of several splinter groups under variously orthodox and questionable episcopal leadership and the national membership continues to plummet as we speak. Though not exactly crashing and burning, the national denominational leadership is fully aware of the crisis. The low esteem placed on discipline reflected in this study is merely another sign of troubled waters for the Episcopal church U.S.A. and, by extension, the Anglican Communion.

At the risk of appearing to belabor the point, a quick look at the statistics maintained by the National Council of churches on denominational member-ships will prove enlightening. In 1940, the Episcopal church U.S.A. had a membership of 1,996,000 and by 1970 it had grown to 3,269,000, that is, a growth of 60%! On the other hand, the 1995 membership figure of "members" rather than "full/confirmed members," stands at 2,536,000, that is, a drop of 23% in twenty-five years, as against an increase of 60% in thirty years. The Episcopal church U.S.A. has not been this small in membership since 1952. Obviously, the two and one-half decades from 1970 to 1995 have been fraught with difficulties and problems for the Protestant traditions in the U.S., as the overall drop in membership shows, but the Episcopal church seems to have fared worse than most in this regard. And, according to recent statistics, there is no relief in sight.

PASTORAL FUNCTIONS

Since Episcopal clergy define themselves at a rate of six in ten as "priests," it was helpful to discover that only in one of the five areas of ministry activities in the Priestly Functions category was stress to be found. Now, with just better than three in ten defining themselves primarily as "pastors," we are pleased to see that, again, only one of the five activities considered in this study is stress-generating for the pastor. That area has to do with involvement in parish life. But first, we should mention that the role of counseling is valued quite highly among both the laity (60%) and the clergy (50%), with only the smallest of percentages (8% and 12% respectively) inclined to value it rather "low."

When it comes to the pastor's involvement in the life of the parish, stress appears. Nearly six in ten (58%) of the parish believe the pastor's time is highly important in discharging this responsibility, while only three in ten (32%) among the clergy have the same feeling. Again, only one in ten members of the parish feel it is of low importance, while better than three in ten (34%) of the clergy mark it "low." Here there is decidedly a divergence of opinion as to the way the pastor should divide up ministry time. Further-more, a point of stress also arises within the clergy ranks as they are divided equally among the three levels of valuation – high importance, low impor-tance, indifferent.

Whereas stress exists in the area of parish involvement, it decidedly does not in the remaining three areas of (1) community involvement (only two in ten of the laity and of the clergy value it), (2) addressing the social, moral, and political issues of the day (only two in ten of the laity and three in ten of the clergy think this an appropriate role for ministry), (3) and nearly four in ten laity and clergy highly rate administrative functions by the pastor as legitimate use of pastoral time. With regards to administration, it should be pointed out in all fairness that the laity seem to be rather equally divided as to whether it is important or not, and so are the clergy.

THE WORK WEEK

The Episcopal clergy settle in right at the middle of these traditions when it comes to the amount of clock time spent weekly in the exercise of ministry with 52 hours, matching the Methodists, falling twelves hours short of Catholic priests and four hours above the Lutherans. If Episcopal clergy match the Methodists for time spent in ministry weekly, they match the Lutherans in the three categories of scholar, priest, and pastor. With 41% of their work week spent in scholarly pursuits, particularly the study of theology and Scripture and sermon preparation, they lead the pack of traditions in our investigation. Their priestly functions take up 26% of their time which falls 14% below the Catholics but matches or betters the Lutherans (26%) and Methodists (25%). Their pastoral portion is 33%, bettering the Catholics by 3% and falling short of both the Methodists (39%) and the Lutherans (34%). It strikes one as problematic that Episcopal clergy would make the conscious decision to direct better than 40% of their ministry time in the scholarly pursuits of theology and Scripture study when they indicate their awareness that the parish does not look favorably upon such priorities. In the final analysis, we would believe that the work week would go better for Episcopal clergy concerned with stress if they concentrated more of their time in the planning and leading of worship, pastoral counseling (and decidedly NOT spiritual direction), and in administering the affairs of the parish and diocesan-related management issues.

STRESS-INDUCERS

As we have noted earlier, the Methodist clergy experience stress-inducing situations in seven of the fifteen ministry activities examined in this study. The Catholics came out with the fewest at three and the Lutherans and Episcopalians tied with four each. However, *only one of the fifteen ministry activities produced stress for all four denominations*, namely, the conflict over the amount of time spent studying Scripture. We have had much to say about this phenomenon already and need only mention it here in passing. In the three categories of ministry – scholarly, priestly, pastoral – the Episcopal clergy had two stress-inducing activities in the first, one in the second, and two in the third. In the first category, "Scholarly Functions," the Episcopal clergy share with the Catholics in encountering conflict over time allocations in both the study of theology and of Scripture, with both traditions showing the laity less inclined, and the clergy more inclined, to value time spent in these activities as important. Across the board, all traditions must do a better job of educating the laity in the value of Scripture study and Anglicans and Catholics must put forth a concerted effort to demonstrate the value of studying theology, both for the effectiveness of preaching, and for professional and spiritual growth of the clergy involved.

Only for the Episcopalians do we find conflict over time spent in spiritual direction as a stress-inducing situation. The laity are by far the least interested in seeing their pastor spend time in such ministry activity, whereas among the Catholics and Lutherans, even among the Methodists, there is an outstanding interest in this ministry. The Episcopal clergy, however, are more nearly in line with their denominational colleagues in all four traditions in terms of the value placed on spiritual direction as a legitimate exercise of ministry and use of pastoral time.

Finally, Episcopal clergy share with Lutherans and Methodists a stress situation over their involvement in the social life of the parish, for in all three traditions the clergy are rather disinclined to be so involved, whereas the laity are rather insistent upon the meaning and value of this ministry activity. We have pointed out earlier that it appears as though the Catholic clergy are exempt from such parish expectations, owing possibly to the Catholic laity's awareness of the shortage of priests and the need for priests to be engaged in the sacramental life of the parish, even if it means less social involvement. For Episcopal laity, next only to the Methodists, this ministry is of major value and considered highly important in pastoral function.

SATISFACTION-INDUCERS

Given the present numerical decline in national membership within the Episcopal church U.S.A., one would have imagined that stress among the clergy would be extremely high. Not so. We found only four stress areas of ministry, and that puts the Anglican clergy right up there with the Lutherans and near the Catholics in terms of overall satisfaction.

This leads us to conclude with a few repetitional remarks regarding satisfaction-inducing situations within parish ministry in the Anglican communion in the United States today as we found it in our study. First, and by far the most impressive, is the fact that of the four activities – sermon preparation, leading public worship, celebrating Eucharist, and exercising sacramental ministries – the Episcopal clergy have an extremely high level of satisfaction, with a low of 78% for the last listed activity and a high of 100% for Eucharist. Without question, the Episcopal church in America today is finding its most fulfilling parish/clergy relationships realized in public liturgical activities – preaching, worshipping, Eucharist, and sacramental ministries. Furthermore, there is mutual consensus between clergy and laity in the Anglican communion that the pastor is not to be particularly concerned with the exercise of ministry functions which involve such things as being a public spokesperson for the church, being an intellectual, per se, certainly not bothering with attempts to exercise discipline, nor bothering with the moral, political, and social issues of the day. Concentrating on matters of worship, pastoral counseling, and administration of the parish will stand the pastor in good stead with the congregation, and this seems to be the long and short of it.

CHAPTER FOUR

COMPARATIVE ANALYSIS
Similarities and Differences in Time Task Data

Now that we have given a fair treatment to each of the respective denominational traditions being considered here, it seems only proper that we attempt
to extract a different set of insights from the data by identifying a variety of
variables which might be compared across denominational lines. It is
important for the integrity of the study to have first allowed each denomination
to stand on its own in terms of a sense of "internal" authenticity of experience.
Comparisons across institutional lines, whether religious, educational,
political, or economic, are usually called into question when there has not first
been an indication of the authenticity of the data uniquely relative to each of
the compared institutions. Here we have attempted to avoid that problem by
providing a thorough going analysis within the framework of each tradition,
allowing that tradition to speak through its own data without quick and ready
reference to outside data. The Methodist experience is unique to that tradition
and, therefore, the data generated should be reflective of that uniqueness. The
same is true of Lutherans and Catholics and, indeed, all religious institutions
and traditions. But to disallow comparisons between and across institutional
lines when those institutions share a common purpose and self-understanding
is to preclude gaining even deeper insight into each of the traditions, as well
as a more refined perception of the institutional phenomenon itself. Though
Methodists are Methodists and not Lutherans, so likewise Lutherans are
Lutherans and not Catholics, but certainly when it comes to matters related to
the profession of ministry and the institutional classification of clergy there is
much held in common across those denominational lines. And even where
there are differences rather than commonalities, the differences are understandable across institutional and traditional lines, nevertheless.

Such is the position taken in this study. A thorough going analysis of each of
the traditions now gives us licenses to pursue an interesting exploration of the
similarities and differences across, rather than within, the traditions under
consideration here.

BIOGRAPHICAL DATA -- Age/Education/Self-Image/Work Week

We will not simply reiterate all of the data discussed in detail in the previous chapter. Rather, we will operate selectively, watching for those points of obvious or outstanding and surprising similarities, as well as differences, among Methodist, Lutheran, Episcopal, and Catholic clergy for the purpose of deepening our understanding and insight into the nature of the profession of ministry as practiced and lived out by ministers in each tradition. It is no surprise to find Catholic clergy older on average than Methodist or Lutheran clergy, if for no other reason than the decline in priestly vocations and attendance at Catholic seminaries during the past twenty years. The average Catholic priest in this study is 56 years of age and left seminary over thirty years ago, whereas the Methodist pastor is 46 years of age and left seminary ten years later with the Lutheran clergy following the Methodist by two years. The Episcopal clergy in the study average 53 years.

The educational level might reflect this difference in age as well -- we would prefer to think of age making the difference rather than being a reflection of the tradition's interest or lack of interest in continuing education for the clergy -- for only one in three (32%) of the Methodist clergy, as compared to four in ten (42%) of the Lutheran and nearly six in ten (58%) of the Catholic clergy, hold advanced graduate degrees in some cognate field of ministry. The Episcopal clergy came in at only 22% holding an advanced degree. Of those holding these advanced degrees, nearly nine out of ten of the Methodist hold the Doctor of Ministry degree, whereas just less than half of the Lutherans hold doctorates and only one in four Catholic and Episcopal priests hold doctorates. Given the age of the priests, it should be pointed out that the most common terminal degree for "older" Catholic priests would be the Licentiate in Sacred Theology rather than a Doctor of Ministry, which is a more recent degree and, until lately, more commonly thought of as Protestant in character. In education, the Episcopal clergy come out on the short end of the stick both in terms of percentages of those who hold a post-ordination degree and of those who hold a doctorate in a cognate field of theology. Given the intellectual tradition of the church of England, one would have thought that the American clergy in the Anglican tradition would have held their ranks high in academic distinction but, as pointed out earlier, even among the bishops there is an extremely low level of academic training.

In all fairness to the data, however, we cannot avoid mentioning that two major stress-inducing areas of ministry function among the Methodist clergy are stress generated by conflict between the pastor and the congregation over time spent in study of Scripture and questions regarding the pastor functioning as a respected intellectual within the community. There does seem to be a tendency towards anti-intellectualism suggested here, for we also found that even in the study of theology, the Methodist clergy receive the lowest approval rating from the congregation of the four traditions being studied, with the Catholic priests receiving the highest affirmations in the categories of study of Scripture, theology, and intellectual involvement in the parish. The fact that nearly six in ten Catholic priests hold advanced degrees seems to corroborate the observation that the Catholic tradition may more readily nurture and foster scholarly activity.

Furthermore, in terms of self-image, we are not surprised to find that nine in ten Methodist and Lutheran clergy think of themselves primarily as "pastor," whereas the Catholic and Episcopal clergy think of themselves primarily as "priest." In keeping with the tradition's emphasis upon the "via media," or middle way between traditional Protestantism and the Roman Catholic church, the Anglican clergy have held true to form by selecting to designate themselves "priests" six out of ten times and only three out of ten times as "pastors" first. The Anglican clergy join the ranks of the other three traditions in abjuring the self-image classification of "scholar." In Chapter Three, when we looked at the percentage of time spent by the clergy in each of the three categories of activity (scholarly, priestly, and pastoral), we found that Catholic priests spend more time (40%) in priestly functions than in any other category, whereas Methodist clergy spend more time in pastoral functions than anywhere else (39%). Lutherans, somewhat interestingly, even though they characterize themselves at a 90% rate as primarily "pastoral," spend more time (40%) in scholarly activities than anywhere else. Here is the first and essentially only time in the analysis of the data that we have found confirmed what was taken as a "domain assumption" during the early formulations of this study, viz., that Methodist are "pastors," Lutherans are "scholars," and Catholics are "priests." Here and only here, in the percentage breakdown of Time Task Allocation, do we find this assumption borne out unquestionably by the research. The actual percentage in order of time spent in the three categories of ministry -- scholarly, priestly, pastoral -- by denomination is as follows: Methodist (Pastoral at 39%; Scholarly at 37%; Priestly at 25%),

Lutheran (Scholarly at 40%; Pastoral at 34%; Priestly at 26%), Catholic (Priestly at 40%; and Scholarly and Pastoral both at 30%), and Episcopal (Priestly at 26%, Scholarly at 33%, Pastoral at 41%).

Finally, in the category of biographical data, the work week of the clergy in each of the traditions is quite interesting in that Catholic priests spend 25% more time per week in ministry activities than do the Lutherans, with the times reported by the clergy themselves as Methodist and Episcopalian (52 hours), Lutheran (48 hours), and Catholic (64 hours).

SCHOLARLY FUNCTIONS

Five areas of activities are considered here -- (1) sermon preparation, (2) study of theology, (3) study of Scripture, (4) clergy as spokespersons for the church, and (5) clergy as respected intellectuals within the parish. In each area, there are interesting points of comparison worthy of our quick recitation and comment. In the matter of sermon preparation, each of the four traditions find their clergy being rather heartily affirmed in their sermon preparation, but Catholic clergy spend only four and a half hours a week in such preparation, whereas the Lutheran clergy spend a full seven hours (with Methodist clergy close behind). Episcopal clergy take the prize with 8.5 hours weekly in sermon preparation.

However, in the area of theological study, we find all denominational clergy spending about the same amount of time at this activity, but where the difference comes is in the realization that a stress-inducing situation exists within the Catholic church because of the great imbalance between the clergy's high valuation of this activity over against the parish's low valuation of theological study. This constitutes only one of three stress-inducing areas of activity for the Catholic clergy and one that is shared with the other denominations when applied to the study of Scripture because, surprisingly, all four denominations find the parish extremely unsupportive of clergy time spent studying Scripture. Surprisingly, only the Episcopal clergy perceive their congregations valuing theological study lower than the others, with only 6% of the laity giving it a high mark. Again, the Episcopal clergy themselves rate theological study lower than any of the other traditions, just slightly lower than the Methodists and more than four times lower than the Lutherans and

Catholics. And only among the Episcopalians is the issue of studying theology a point of stress rather than, as with the other traditions, a point of satisfaction in time-task allocation in ministry function.

Stress is created between the clergy and the congregation in all four churches over what one would have imagined to be a rather safe area of agreement, viz., studying Scripture. *How surprising that conflict between clergy and parish over Scripture study would be the one and only ministry activity in which all four denominations create stress!* Adding astonishment to surprise, we find that the laity in both the Methodist and Lutheran traditions place a lower valuation (only 20% and 22% respectively give Scripture study a high ranking) upon their clergy studying Scripture than do the Catholics with 28% ranking it at the high mark. We are so surprised, it seems, because the two traditions which have grown out of the *sola Scriptura* position regarding faith and practice have valued the study of Scripture lower than have the Catholics who look to the church as the source of authority in matters of faith and practice. Either the Methodists and Lutherans are doing a poor job of emphasizing the importance of Scripture study for the clergy or the Catholic church has done an admirable job in educating the laity to value scripture study by the clergy. Certainly, there is much to be found out about this striking phenomenon before the final verdict is in, but no one will argue that it is uninteresting. What the Episcopalians do hold in common with the other three traditions is the fact that stress is generated between pastor and parish over the study of Scripture! Of the many surprise findings in this study, this ranks among one of the most outstanding. Who would have imagined that the conflict generated over issues of time allocation would be consistently evidenced across all four denominations when it comes to the study of Scripture? More than twice as many Episcopal clergy highly value Scripture study as do members of their parishes.

Again, in the scholarly function of ministry having to do with the clergy serving as spokespersons for the teachings of the church, all four denominations are more or less in agreement as to valuation by both clergy and laity. All that can be reported by way of comparison and contrast is that Catholic clergy spend four hours at such matters where as Methodist, Lutheran and Episcopal clergy spend less than three hours. Again, the Episcopalians have the distinction of placing the least value on the pastor serving as a spokesperson by a substantial margin, both among the clergy and among the laity. The Methodists and Catholics more than twice as often value highly this function.

Finally, the issue of the pastor functioning as a respected intellectual in the life of the parish has been a case for stress among the Methodist clergy. Only among the Lutheran clergy, surprisingly, do we find the pastor as intellectual valued lower than among the Episcopal clergy. However, Episcopal laity value the pastor's function as intellectual higher than any of the other three groups of laity, leading us to wonder about the contrast in self-image between the Episcopal clergy, who are disinclined to assume the role of intellectual, whereas the Episcopal laity value its function in the parish.

PRIESTLY FUNCTIONS

The Catholic clergy, as mentioned earlier, feel more at home with the "priestly" description than do the Methodist or Lutheran clergy (Episcopal clergy are somewhat more comfortable with it) and the percentage of time spent discharging these five areas of priestly ministry bear that out. Catholic clergy spend 40% of their time here, whereas the Methodists only 25% and the Lutherans and Episcopalians close behind at 26%. The five activities are (1) leading the public worship, (2) presiding at Communion, (3) exercising other sacramental ministries, (4) serving as spiritual director, and (5) administering ecclesiastical discipline within the parish.

Across the board, all four traditions receive a high level of affirmation from the laity with regard to leading the congregation in worship. If nothing more can be learned here than this, we can agree that we have reaffirmed the church's belief that public worship is what the laity most need and most seek from their clergy. The only interesting variant in the data has to do with the amount of time spent in this activity -- the Protestants at three hours a week and the Catholics at eight and one-quarter hour weekly. Lower than the laity of the Lutherans and Catholics and equal with the Methodists, the Episcopal laity value the pastor as leader of public worship. Only the Methodist fall below the Episcopal clergy, however, in their value of this function and they tie the Lutherans, but are surpassed by the Catholics in this ministry of public worship.

When it comes to presiding at the Lord's Table, the numbers are mixed along denominational lines. In no activity considered in this study do we find a 100% approval of a high valuation by both clergy and laity, other than among the Catholics when it comes to presiding at the Eucharist, for all are in complete agreement as to the centrality of this function to the life of the faithful. And, over eight hours a week are spent in celebrating Eucharist within the Catholic Church, whereas with the Methodists, as well as with the Lutherans, there is on average two hours spent in such activity. With regard to the Eucharist, the Episcopal clergy tie the Catholic clergy in their valuation of this function and the Episcopal laity surpass the Methodists and the Lutherans in their valuation. And similarly, the Episcopal clergy and laity both agree in their high valuation of sacramental ministries of the pastor, surpassing the Lutherans and Methodists and falling just short of Catholic clergy and laity in this regard. Furthermore, we find that for the Methodist, stress is induced because only four in ten Methodist laity give a high mark to this function, while over seven in ten Methodist clergy so rank it, thereby creating stress over the conflict between the six in ten Methodist laity who value presiding at Table low against the seven in ten clergy who value it highly.

In the area of sacramental ministries (such as baptisms, etc.), no stress is produced in any of the   denominations; however, there is a detectable acceleration of affirmation moving from the Methodist laity (at only 36% laity and 40% clergy), to the Lutherans (at 64% laity and clergy), and finally, to the Catholics (at 84% for clergy and laity). Sacramental ministries other than Eucharist seem not to be of value to the Protestant tradition in the same manner or to the same degree as for Catholics.

However, the same cannot be said of spiritual direction as a ministry function. Three of the traditions value the ministry of spiritual direction at almost exactly the same percentage among both the clergy and the laity, and this is quite surprising, given the very recent willingness to consider spirituality issues as a focus of ministry within the Protestant traditions. Having thrown so much of the spiritual tradition of the church away during and immediately following the onset of the Reformation, the Protestant churches have begun to systematically reappropriate their Catholic heritage and spirituality, spiritual formation, and spiritual direction, the arena in which the Protestant clergy and laity are most active. Spiritual direction among the Episcopalians, both clergy and laity, fares poorly compared to the other three traditions. The clergy within all three of the other traditions place a higher value on spiritual direction than do the Episcopal clergy, and among the laity the contrast is even more stark, with nearly twice as many Methodists and Catholics and nearly three times as many Lutherans valuing spiritual direction higher than do the Episcopal laity. Given the rich spiritual tradition of Anglicanism, the clergy have their work cut out for them in this regard.

Finally, in the area of priestly functions, we have a striking surprise, viz., it appears as though the Lutherans are more interested in, and approving of, the use of ecclesiastical discipline than are either the Methodists (only 2% of the laity and 28% of the clergy approve) or the Catholics (only 9% of the laity and 18% of the clergy approve), whereas the Lutherans approve at an astounding rate of 28% for the laity and 34% for the clergy. There is virtually no approval among the Episcopalians, clergy or laity! It could be argued here, and at the risk, it might be pointed out, of garnering the wrath of the Lutheran church in the process, that the Lutherans are particularly anxious to employ the use of ecclesiastical discipline in an attempt to establish some form of jurisdiction for and by the church in deference to the Catholic doctrine of the Magisterium. However, the Lutherans are at a loss to determine, for sure, the basis of authority and discipline, since the tradition still adheres to a *sola Scriptura* doctrine regarding faith and practice. In the absence of the traditions of Christianity as established and perpetrated by the Catholic church, the Lutherans are left with a mixed bag of local autonomy and national identity.

Finally, it should be pointed out that the Methodists have once again allowed themselves to create a stress situation regarding discipline because of the wide disparity between the feelings of the laity about this matter (only 2% approves) and that of the clergy (with 28% approving). For the Methodists, this is a problem that will not easily go away. The Episcopal clergy's sense of responsibility regarding discipline and the exercise of ecclesiastical authority in matters of faith and practice is quite strikingly at variance with the other three traditions. Methodist and Lutheran clergy, at a rate of five times as great, value this function and the Catholic clergy at three times the rate the Episcopal clergy value it. This bespeaks the problem discussed earlier regarding the Episcopal church U.S.A.'s sense of ecclesiastical authority, and issues related to the ordination of women and liturgical reform merely reflect the larger problem. In the absence of any genuine sense of universal conformity in matters of faith and practice, and with the total absence of any mechanism of enforcement of denominational jurisdiction in matters of discipline, the Episcopal church in the U.S. is, strictly speaking, left to its own devices, where any one bishop or priest can hold any given position in matters of faith and practice without fear of the exercise of censorial jurisdiction within the denomination. The "High church" tradition particularly seems to be adrift in these matters, for while claiming to be "Anglo-Catholic" in faith and practice, there is the conspicuous absence of the Magisterium and papal authority.

PASTORAL FUNCTIONS

We have already determined that the Protestant clergy feel much more comfortable with this description of their overall ministry, while the Catholic clergy prefer "priest" as their self-image. That has been reflected in the percentage of time the clergy spend discharging priestly functions. In the area of pastoral function we find a similar trend, for Methodist clergy spend 39% of their time here, with Lutherans spending 34% of their time, while Catholic clergy spend only 30%. The five areas of activity classified as "pastoral function" are (1) pastoral counseling, (2) involvement in the social life of the parish, (3) involvement in the social life of the outside community, (4) addressing the social, moral, and political issues of the day, and (5) in ecclesiastical administration. Selection of activity areas for the pastoral function will cause the greatest amount of discussion and, to be sure, discontentment as to the limitations placed on the list by keeping to the number of five. However, the choices were made and were adhered to and the findings were not disappointing.

All four traditions seem to value pastoral counseling more or less equally among both the clergy and the laity. The most we learned here was that the percentages of clergy and laity who gave a high mark versus a low mark to this ministry were about equally divided. Thus, it is not a truism that all of the laity and all of the clergy enjoy a grand celebration of the centrality of pastoral counseling as a major focus of ministry. Rather, only about half actually do. In point of fact, a much larger percentage of clergy and laity in three of the traditions value "spiritual direction" more highly than "pastoral counseling." Only the Episcopalians are the exception in this. If nothing else, this should give pause for thought to seminary faculty and those in charge of curricula development, both in Protestant and Catholic institutions.

When we come to the pastor's involvement in the social life of the parish, we find that the Protestant traditions experience a stress-inducing situation owing to the disparity between the valuations of the clergy and laity. What is even more telling is that in most instances it is the laity who are more likely to value highly this ministry and the clergy more commonly devalue its importance. Catholic clergy and laity seem to more or less agree that it is of value to the role of ministry in the parish. Interestingly enough, other than in matters related to the valuation placed on Scripture study (where we find all four traditions generating stress for the pastor), only in the matter of the pastor's involvement in the social life of the parish and in the matter of the pastor's involvement in the social issues of the day, do we find as many as three of the four traditions sharing a stress-generating attitude about ministry functions. Three of the four traditions generate stress over this issue, which leads us to believe that during the next decade this will be a major point of concern and development in parish/pastor relations. In every instance, the laity are much more desirous of the pastor's involvement than the pastor is. The Episcopal clergy again distinguish themselves from the other clergy groups in that they have the *smallest percentage* of their ranks who value highly the social involvement in the life of the community outside the parish and, conversely, the Episcopal laity have the *largest percentage* of their ranks who value highly such involvement. It appears that whereas the Episcopal laity wish their pastors to be more involved in the outside community, the pastors prefer less involvement.

With regard to a similar involvement in the social life of the outside community, i.e., outside the parish setting, Methodists and Catholics seem likely to value this ministry rather low, but among the Lutherans there is a stress situation between pastor and parish owing to the former's heightened valuation of this ministry, while the latter rather decidedly devalue such involvement. The trend has been consistent among the Lutherans and there the emphasis seems always to be on ministry and service to the parish at the expense of ministry and service to the community. This creates stress for the pastor who would prefer to be more favorably involved in outside ministry.

This trend among Lutherans continues when we get to considerations of social, moral, and political issues of the day, for with Lutherans, but also with Methodists and Catholics, there is a strong disinterest in such activity on the part of the laity, while there is a much stronger interest on the part of the clergy in addressing such issues publicly. These three denominations have created for themselves a stress-inducing situation for the clergy, owing to this radically divergent view of the meaning and nature of addressing social issues as a manifestation of Christian responsibility and pastoral ministry. The Lutherans, it should be pointed out, have by far the lowest approval rating (4%) on the part of the laity of the other traditions. The Episcopalians come out ahead of the other three traditions when it comes to valuing the pastor's time in being involved in the moral, political, and social issues of the day. Only the Lutherans have a smaller percentage of their clergy who wish not to be involved in speaking out on such issues, whereas the Anglican laity far exceed the other three denominations in their high valuation of such ministry.

Finally, only the Methodists seem to create stress in the parish for the pastor over the laity's consistent devaluation of time spent in the administration of the parish and denomination, even though Methodist clergy spend nearly seven hours a week in such activity. Nearly 40% of the Methodist clergy's time out of a typical work week is taken up in administration, while only 30% of Catholic time is so spent, with the Lutherans falling midway between at 34%. The Episcopalians are at 33%. Where there is a stress-inducing situation in the parish, there is a call for more education at the point of conflict. In this instance, it is patently clear that the Methodist laity, more so than among Lutherans, Episcopalians, and Catholics, seem not to appreciate the importance of this ministry. Given the historic emphasis within the Methodist tradition on personal experience of faith and with a less aggressive sense of institutionalization of the faith-community, it is quite understandable that Methodist laity would feel that "merely" administrative work by the clergy is a less effective use of ministry time than, say, engaging in pastoral counseling or sermon preparation.

On the other hand, among Catholics there seems to be generally a widely accepted feeling that the administration of the parish and diocesan affairs is, indeed, quite appropriately the domain of the priest's function and that time spent in these activities is time spent in the discharge of pastoral responsibility. As numbers of priests continue to decline and numbers of laity continue to increase, there will need to be a more reasoned consideration and evaluation of this perception of effective use of the priest's time. Historically, the deaconate functioned as the administrative arm of the parish and diocese, thereby freeing the priest to engage in specifically "sacramental" ministries. This shift in parish consciousness is imperative and inevitable. Episcopal clergy are at the median when it comes to discharging administrative time, with 33% of their weekly schedule involved in such activities, with 26% involved in priestly functions and 41% in pastoral functions. Also, spending 52 hours for a regular work week places them at the median in this regard as well.

THE WORK WEEK

We have already had a great deal to say about the time clergy spend during the work week discharging their duties. We noted earlier that the Catholic priests spend by far the greatest amount of time "on the job" with a reported average of 64 hours, making, by any standards, for a long week. Lutherans spend the least amount of time at 48 hours with Methodists and Anglicans spending 52 hours each. Again, we must be reminded that these are "reported" times and our interest is not so much in the truth (as if that could ever really be found out in such matters) but in the "perception of reality" by the clergy. If a priest thinks of himself and is convinced that he, indeed, is regularly spending 64 hours a week in ministry, then whether or not that is actually and verifiably true is of little importance. What is important is the fact that he perceives himself spending that amount of time. And, in turn, that perception of reality will directly affect his assessment of the demands of ministry, and eventually, will directly affect his behavior in the role as minister.

Earlier in this study we expressed concern regarding the large number of hours spent in ministry during the average work week by the clergy, by far greater than in the secular world. No one even came close to the accepted 40 hour work week – the Lutherans being nearest that magic number but even they spend an additional eight hours (another full work day). The fatigue factor must eventually be taken into account and a major data-based study of physical and emotional exhaustion brought on by such long hours is crying out to be done. How can communities of faith expect to be well served by sensitive and responsive clergy who are suffering from time-based exhaustion? There is something of the nature of those who are called to ministry which leads them unwittingly into this kind of exhaustion under the false illusion that (1) they are indispensable to the well-being of the community, and (2) only they can do the work of ministry. This leads to a Messiah complex which often devolves into a persecution complex with its attendant cynicism and negativity. Burnout is the ultimate expression of this time-based tension and the phenomenon is on the rise throughout all major denominations.

We could speculate as to the long term positive effects on ministry and communities of faith if the clergy would demand and see to it that they have sufficient leisure time as to nurture and recreate their hearts, minds, and souls. A rested clergy might be just what communities need and are unaware of it. How refreshing it would be to find the pastor rested and ready to serve when called upon without the too common feeling that one is impinging upon the pastor's busy schedule! Why not declare a moratorium on busy schedules? Emotional and physical health, to say nothing of spiritual health, would certainly improve for the clergy if they were to demand a shorter work day and week and deliberately seek out leisure and recreation. This will require a sustained effort at parish education, but it can be done. Nothing bespeaks professional insecurity louder than the professional who refuses to take time off and away from the work place for personal enrichment. Instead of demonstrating to the parish how indispensable the pastor is by always "being on the job," pastors may too often leave the impression with their community that they are "too busy" to bother with them or are undisciplined in scheduling their daily affairs. Longer hours doesn't necessarily mean better ministry for the pastor or for the parish.

We have already reported that Methodist clergy spend 37% of the work week doing scholarly things, 25% doing priestly things, and 39% being pastoral. Lutherans had rather spend 40% of their time as scholars with 26% of their time being priestly and 34% being pastoral. Catholic priests spend much less time being scholarly at 30% of the work week but 40% being priestly balanced by a meager 30% as pastors. The Episcopal clergy come closer to the Lutherans than they do either Methodists or Catholics with 41% being scholarly, 26% being priestly, and 33% being pastoral. The widest disparity of time allocations is between the Methodists (25%) and the Catholics (40%) in the area of priestly activities. The area of greatest commonality is that of pastoral functions with only a 9% variance among the four traditions.

STRESS-INDUCERS -- Common and Distinctive

By way of summary and convenience of grouping, we will take a moment to identify again those stress-inducing situations which are held in common across denominational lines and those which are singularly distinctive of a particular tradition. These common and distinctive stressers have been pointed out intermittently throughout the study, but to group them now after having discussed them in some detail seems appropriate.

In the area of commonly experienced stress-inducing situations within all four traditions, there are three which stand out, viz., (1) the study of Scripture, (2) involvement in the social life of the parish, and (3) addressing social, moral, and political issues. All four denominations more or less generate stress over each of these three activities and in all three, without exception, it is the laity who place a low ranking of importance on them, while the clergy, across the board, place a high mark of importance. We have had much to say about each of these activities, particularly within the context of each of their denominational settings. To group them as commonly held positions across denominational lines seems not to aid in deepening our understanding of the cause of this stress-inducing perception. That stress is generated, and that conflict necessarily exists, is clearly borne out by the data.

Distinctive rather than common stress-inducing situations to each of the denominations has proven more interesting and telling. Among the Catholics, there is only one clearly distinct instance of a stress-creating situation, and that is over the issue of the pastor spending time studying contemporary theology. (The Episcopal clergy share this experience.) That the Catholic laity think little of this enterprise, whereas priests think it quite important, calls for a concerted effort on the part of the clergy to inform and instruct the laity on the meaning and nature of such study and its significance to the ongoing vitality of the priests' ministry. A distinctive stress-inducer within the Lutheran tradition has to do with the pastor's involvement in the social life of the outside community, an activity greatly devalued by the laity but much valued by the clergy. Again, more instruction of the parish on the meaning and nature of this activity as it is a manifestation of the pastor's role to evangelize and witness to the faith in the world is obviously required here, and, using a different tact, to challenge the parish to be less selfish with the pastor's time and more giving and generous towards the community. This Lutheran tendency to see the pastor as "for the parish" rather than as "for the world" has been a consistent finding.

Four stress-inducing situations we have found to be distinctively Methodist in character are, namely, (1) the pastor as intellectual, (2) presiding at Holy Communion, (3) ecclesiastical discipline, and (4) administration. In every instance, the stress is created due to the laity's low estimation of these particular forms of ministry and the pastors' high valuation of their importance in the overall exercise of ministry. That the intellectual flavor of the clergy has not been a distinctive characteristic of the Methodist tradition is well established, but the pastor is today called upon more than ever to display an awareness of the affairs of the world and to demonstrate an acquaintance with the flow of public information. This trend and its importance must somehow be conveyed to the parish such that the laity become supportive of the pastor's desire to participate in the intellectual activity of the community. Methodist clergy's low showing as to holding advanced degrees in theology and ministry (only the Episcopal clergy are lower) seems to be reflective of this tendency within the tradition to down-play scholarship generally.

The devaluation of the time spent in presiding at the Lord's Table on the part of the Methodist laity, while the clergy find themselves increasingly valuing this activity highly, might be suggestive of the still strong "Protestant" notion about the Eucharist among the laity and a growing sense of "catholicity" regarding Communion among the clergy. Bringing Holy Communion into the central arena of the parish's worship life within Methodism is a recent development and has been initiated by the clergy rather than the laity. Whereas the sermon seems to be the focus of the congregation (72% rank it high), the Eucharist seems to be the increasing focus of the clergy (74% rank it high).

Another stresser for the Methodist clergy is the difference of opinion with respect to the meaning and nature of the exercise of ecclesiastical discipline, and this problem will not go away, since the core of the problem centers around the problematics of a balance between "*sola Scriptura*" and "personal piety." These two emphases within the tradition preclude any strong sense of the meaningfulness and, indeed, rightfulness of discipline of any kind being administered by the clergy upon the laity. Finally, the matter of administration will be an enduring struggle between the laity (concerned with local parish life) and the clergy (concerned with the management of the institutional church locally and nationally).

SATISFACTION-INDUCERS -- Common and Distinctive

This component of our study naturally has proven the most pleasing for the identification of causes of satisfaction within the parish on the part of the clergy is, indeed, a worthy enterprise. And we found five common satisfaction-inducers across denominational lines. They are (1) sermon preparation, (2) serving as the church's spokesperson, (3) leading the public worship, (4) spiritual direction (with the exception of the Episcopalians), and (5) pastoral counseling. Clearly these are the areas among Protestants and Catholics, laity and clergy alike, where there will be mutual agreement, generally speaking, as to the high valuation allocated for ministry -- preaching, witnessing, worshipping, and spiritual and pastoral guidance.

That pastors do themselves and their parishes a great service directly in proportion to the amount of time allocated for these five primary functions goes without saying. We would suggest that in most cases where stress is being generated in the parish setting, the pastor and the congregation would be well served if these five activities were to be accentuated.

The *distinctive* satisfaction-inducers were less clear among the Protestants, none showing up in the data for the Methodist tradition and only one for the Lutherans. When we remember that seven out of fifteen activities were stress-inducing for Methodist clergy, whereas for Lutherans and Episcopalians only four and Catholics only three, we should have anticipated that satisfying situations would be less likely distinctive to the Methodist tradition than to the other three. For Lutherans and Episcopalians, the highest single activity of satisfaction not held in common with the other two traditions was that of presiding at the Eucharist (which they shared with Catholics but not Methodists). This reflects a growing sense of "catholicity" among the Lutheran and Episcopal church leaders and laity in America and the trend will certainly continue. *Distinctive* satisfaction-inducing situations for the Catholics number three and they include (1) presiding at the Eucharist (shared with Lutherans but not Methodists), (2) sacramental ministries other than Eucharist, and (3) involvement in the social life of the parish. These three activities are historically characteristic of Catholic clergy and today the level of satisfaction between clergy and laity in these three areas proves to be a distinctive mark of the relationship which exists between the priest and the parish in the Catholic church. It is a source of strength and hope for the future.

CONCLUDING REMARKS

When doing data-based studies of interesting topics in which fascinating and provocative information is gathered and analyzed that offers new and better insights into the subject under scrutiny, there is always the tendency to speak and write in superlatives. This author is fully aware of this danger and, on occasion, has been known to fall victim to that mind set.

When it comes to a contemporary understanding of the nature and meaning of ministry in the closing days of the 20th century, we must exercise care, yet not be reluctant, in the use of superlatives if the insights gained from such studies as this one merits them. Few will argue, I believe, that the present state of the clergy is in a massive transition period of redefinition and new understanding both of itself and the nature of its place and function in the life of the church.

It is unfair of us, on the basis of this one study, to attempt to pontificate as to the full scope of ministry in today's church. We have studied four thousand randomly selected clergy divided equally among four major Christian traditions. That which has caught and sustained our attention throughout this study has been those activities of ministry which are perceived by the clergy themselves to be stress inducing and, happily, those which are satisfaction inducing. We have attempted to highlight problem areas in order both to deepen our understanding of the problems and to hopefully provide relevant information for those in decision-making positions of power and leadership upon which to act.

Several major problems across the board have presented themselves to us, such as the need for communities of faith to be better informed and educated as to the nature and function of ministry and the relevance of such activities as studying Scripture and theology, and, in many instances, the need for the community to better appreciate the relevance of clergy activity in the wider world beyond the parish. But one of the most striking and consistently troubling phenomena gleaned from this study has been the quite obvious reality of the overworked clergy. That is to say, clergy are quite obviously spending too many hours on the job discharging too many duties with too many stresses and frustrations, many brought on by their own perceptions of parish expectations and in others by their own self-understanding as to the nature of ministry. Whatever the cause clergy exhaustion – physical, emotional, spiritual – is a problem that will not go away easily and must be addressed by both the lay and clerical communities alike. Whether suffering from a messiah complex (I must save the world) or from an anxiety about job security (I must keep proving myself), the problem is real and pervasive.

Throughout the book, we have endeavored to make clear the fact that what is being discovered in these data are "clergy perceptions" rather than either perceptions of and by the laity or insights gained by an objective gleaning of parish-based responses. The issue before us from the outset has been "clergy perceptions" of these various ministry activities since their perceptions determine their outlook on their communities and their ministries.

Other studies might be done in which the parish itself is asked to address the same and similar questions regarding their own understanding of ministry and their expectations regarding their clergy. It would be, indeed, a worthwhile endeavor. Yet, nevertheless, it would be quite different from what we set out to do and the findings may or may not corroborate ours here. But in closing, let us be clear in what we have done. We have asked the clergy to tell us what they do with their time and how they evaluate those doings in terms of priorities, and, secondly, we have asked them to share with us what they think their communities of faith think and feel about those same activities in terms of priorities. If we have done this, we have fulfilled our goal. If not, it still needs to be done.

BIBLIOGRAPHICAL RESOURCES

DATA-BASED REFERENCE

Yearbook of American and Canadian church 1997 edited by Kenneth B. Bedell, published and distributed by Abingdon Press Nashville and prepared and edited for the Communication Commission of the National Council of the churches of Christ in the U.S.A., 475 Riverside Drive, New York, NY 10115-0050.

MAJOR WORKS IN THE FIELD OF RELEVANCE TO OUR STUDY

One of the most outstanding books written in this decade addressed to the issue of priestly vocation and the theological meaning of ministry in the modern church has been written by Avery Dulles, S.J., *THE PRIESTLY OFFICE: A Theological Reflection*, New York: Paulist Press, 1997. The book consists of the five lectures delivered at the National Institute for Clergy Formation at Seton Hall University in June of 1996. The focus of the essays is upon the subject of the ordained priesthood in the light of Vatican II and recent magisterial and theological teaching.

Another significant source of major scholarship is the *SEMINARY JOURNAL*, published by the National Catholic Education Association, and particularly helpful in the writing of this book were essays in two numbers of Volume II, Winter 1996, #2 and #3. The report of Rev. James J. Walsh, director of the Seminary Department of the NCEA entiled, "MATS in Transition! Report on Annual Meeting of the Midwest Association of Theological Schools," and an article by the Rev. Ernest Skublics, "Priests or Pastors: Is It a Real Dilemma?" Father Skublics is the Academic Dean of Mount Angel Seminary and the article was in response to a previous article in the *SEMINARY JOURNAL* by Father Gary Riebe-Estrella entitled, "American Cultural Shifts: Formation for Which Candidates? For Which Church?" Father Riebe-Estrella is Academic Dean of the Catholic Theological Union in Chicago. Both the article and the response were significantly important in early consideration for the writing of this study. Another article of relevance in the same issue of *SJ*, II, #2, was by

Father Philip J. Murnion entitled, "Culture, Priesthood and Ministry: The Priest for the New Millennium."

A recent collection of stimulating essays under the co-editorship of Robert R. Lutz and Bruce T. Taylor entitled, *SURVIVING IN MINISTRY: Navigating the Pitfalls, Experience the Renewals* by Integration Books/Paulist Press, 1990, proved helpful early on in these deliberations, with particular attention being given to Rea McDonnell, SSND, and her essay entitled, "The Spiritual Life of the Ministry." An interesting book from the Protestant perspective has been done by a Hartford Seminary professor, Jackson W. Carroll, entitled, *AS ONE WITH AUTHORITY: Reflective Leadership in Ministry* published by Westminster/John Knox Press, 1991. For Catholics, the book is an interesting insight into the problematics of authority in the absence of a Magisterium and the teaching office of the church as understood in the Catholic church. He wrestles with the dynamics of decision-making and leadership and it is quite well done.

From the Anglican side of these, there are two major classics, without which no discussion of the priesthood and ministry would be complete. The first is by R. C. Moberly, late Regius Professor of Pastoral Theology in the University of Oxford and a Canon of Christ Church/Oxford from 1892 to 1903. The book is entitled, *MINISTERIAL PRIESTHOOD: Chapters on the Rationale of Ministry and the Meaning of Christian Priesthood*, published by London: S.P.C.K., 1969, in reprint form. It is outstanding and is Anglicanism and Oxford scholarship at its very best. Additionally, and in the same genre of scholarship and Anglican Churchmanship, is a collection of essays prepared under the direction of Kenneth E. Kirk, then Bishop of Oxford, entitled, *THE APOSTOLIC MINISTRY: Essays on the History and the Doctrine of Episcopacy*, published by New York: Morehouse-Gorham, 1946. An excerpt from the Foreword will illustrate the depth of consideration evidenced in this distinguished collection of Anglican theologians. "The view that the traditional doctrine of the episcopate is wholly discontinuous from anything contained in the New Testament -- especially from our Lord's call and commissioning of His apostles -- was first clearly asserted in Hatch's Bampton Lectures of 1880, in which the origins of episcopacy were sought in the episcopi of pagan clubs and societies. It reappeared in Harnack's theory of the 'charismatic' ... These essays have been prepared in an effort by their authors to understand for themselves, and to set out for the consideration of others, both of the same communion and of other traditions, how far episcopacy has been a primary determinant of that which they have received. They are bound to ask themselves, quite frankly, whether, after all, episcopay is essential to the continuous integrity of the Gospel of Christ throughout the ages; and if so, in what respects it is essential; what elements in the traditional form in which it has appeared must be retained at all costs, and what elements can be or ought to be discarded for the removal of difficulties and the right solution of problems. That they have made some contribution towards an agreed answer to such questions as these is the deepest hope of those whose names appear on the title page of this volume." Without doubt, the most outstanding essays in this collection of essays are those presented by Bishop Kenneth Kirk himself, "The Apostolic Ministry," and by the Rev. A. G. Hebert of the Society of the Sacred Mission entitled, "Ministerial Episcopacy." No investigation of, or appreciation for, the self-understanding of priesthood within the Anglican Communion will be complete without carefully and thoughtfully engaging this collection of essays.

W. Clark Gilpin of the University of Chicago has written an outstanding investigation of the meaning of the theological task today (for Protestantism) in a little soon-to-be-judged classic entitled, *A PREFACE TO THEOLOGY* published by the University of Chicago Press, 1996. "What do theologians do?" is his opening question and his consideration of Protestant theological training in American seminaries, past and present, is most insightful. A significant collection of essays dealing with the historic ministry in the writings of the early Fathers has been nicely edited by Philip L. Culbertson and Arthur Bradford Shippee entitled, THE PASTOR: Readings from the Patristic Period and published by Fortress Press, 1990. And finally, for a study of the history of the priesthood in the Catholic church, there is no better source today than that done by Kenan B. Osborne, OFM, entitled, *PRIESTHOOD: A History of Ordained Ministry in the Roman Catholic Church,* published by Paulist Press, 1988. In a word, it is "indispensable" for any serious discussion of Catholic priesthood, past or present. It is rich with knowledge of the early Fathers and subsequent generations of the church's teaching on ministry up to, and including, a reasoned assessment of things as they presently stand since Vatican II and matters related to ecumenical relationships affecting a theology of priesthood.

94   John H. Morgan

RESOURCE BIBLIOGRAPHY IN THE FIELD OF MINISTRY

Hans Ursvon Balthasar, "The Priest of the New Covenant," in his *Explorations in Theology IV.* Spirit and Institution (San Francisco: Ignatius, 1995).

Peter L. Berger, *The Sacred Canopy* (N.Y.: Doubleday, 1967).

Peter L. Berger, *The Social Construction of Reality* (N.Y.: Doubleday, 1966).

Burton J. Bledstein, *The Culture of Professionalism* (N.Y.: W.W. Norton, 1976).

Samuel W. Blizzard, *The Protestant Parish Minister: A Behavioral Science Interpretation.* Society for the Scientific Study of Religion Monograph Series, no. 5. Storrs, CT.: Society for the Scientific Study of Religion, 1985.

Leonardo Boff, *Ecclesiogenesis: The Base Communities Reinvent the Church* (Maryknoll, N.Y..: Orbis, 1986).

Patrick J. Brennan, *The Evangelizing Parish: Theologies and Strategies for Renewal* (Allen, TX.: Tabor, 1987).

Raymond E. Brown, *Priest and Bishop: Biblical Reflections* (N.Y.: Paulist Press, 1970).

Don S. Browning, "Integrating the Approaches: A Practical Theology," in *Building Effective Ministry,* edited by Carl S. Dudley (San Francisco: Harper & Row, 1983).

Jackson W. Carroll, *Ministry as Reflective Practice.* Washington, D.C.: The Alban Institute, 1986.

Jackson W. Carroll, "Some Issues in Clergy Authority," in *Review of Religious Research* 23: 99-117.

Jackson W. Carroll, "The Congregation as Chameleon: How the Past Interprets the Present," in *Congregations: Their Power to Form and Transform*, edited by C. Ellis Nelson (Atlanta: John Knox Press, 1988).

David Foy Crabtree, *The Empowering Church* (Washington, D.C.: The Alban Institute, 1989).

Fred Craddock, *As One Without Authority* (Nashville: Abingdon Press, 1979).

Daniel Donovan, *What Are They Saying about Ministerial Priesthood?* (N.Y.: Paulist Press, 1992).

Jane Dempsey Douglass, "A Study of the Congregation in History," in *Beyond Clericalism: The Congregation as a Focus for Theological Education*, edited by Joseph C. Hough, Jr., and Barbara G. Wheeler (Atlanta: Scholars Press, 1988).

Avery Dulles, S.J., *Models of the Church* (Garden City, N.Y.: Doubleday, 1978).

Avery Dulles, S.J., "The Protestant Minister and the Prophetic Mission," in *Theological Studies* 21(1960).

Avery Dulles, S.J., *A Church to Believe In* (N.Y.: Crossroad, 1983).

Jean Galot, *Theology of the Priesthood* (San Francisco: Ignatius, 1984).

James M. Gustafson, "Professions as Callings," in *The Social Service Review* 56:501-515, 1982.

Paul M. Harrison, *Authority and Power in the Free Church Tradition* (Princeton, N.J.: Princeton University Press, 1980).

Urban Holmes, *The Priest in Community* (N.Y.: Seabury Press, 1978).

Joseph C. Hough, Jr., and John B. Cobb, Jr., *Christian Identity and Theological Education* (Atlanta: Scholars Press, 1985).

96   John H. Morgan

James D. Hunter, *American Evangelicalism: Conservative Religion and the Quandary of Modernity* (New Brunswick, N.J.: Rugters University Press, 1983).

Martha L. Ice, *Clergywomen and Their Worldviews* (New York: Praeger Publs., 1987).

John H. Morgan, *Catholic Spirituality: A Guide for Protestants* (Bristol, IN: Wyndham Hall Press, 1995).

John Paul II, "The Example of St. John Vianney," *Origins* 15 (April 3, 1986): 685-691.

------------, *Crossing the Threshold of Hope* (N.Y.: Knopf, 1994).

------------, *Apostolic Exhortation **Pastores dabo vobis**,* 27-30 (Washington, D.C.:United States Catholic Conference, 1992), pp. 71-81.

------------, *Encyclical **Redemptoris** mission,* 67; text in *Origins* 20 (January 31, 1991): 541-68.

------------, "A Vision of the Priest's Role," *Origins* 8 (February 15, 1979): 547-49.

------------, "Apostolic Exhortation on ⁻⁻con. iliation and Penance" 29; *Origins* 14 (December 20, 1984): 432-58.

------------, Holy Thursday Letter ***Dominicae cenae*** 2; text in Kilmartin (below).

Walter Kasper, "A New Dogmatic Outlook on the Priestly Ministry," *Concilium* 43, *The Identity of the Priest* (N.Y.: Paulist, 1969), 20-33.

David H. Kelsey, *The Uses of Scripture in Recent Theology* (Philadelphia: Fortress Press, 1975).

Edward Kilmartin, *Church, Eucharist, and Priesthood* (N.Y.: Paulist, 1981).

Sherryl Kleinman, *Equals Before God: Seminarians as Humanistic Professionals* (Chicago: University of Chicago Press, 1984).

Hans Kung, *Why Priests?* (Garden City, N.Y.: Doubleday, 1972). For balance see "Vatican Declaration on Hans Kung," *Origins* 4 (March 6, 1975): 577-579.

Magali S. Larson, *The Rise of Professionalism: A Sociological Analysis* (Berkeley, CA.: University of California Press, 1977).

Lutheran Church in America, God's People in Ministry (Philadelphia: Division for Professional Leadership, 1984).

Sidney Mead, "The Rise of the Evangelical Conception of Ministry in America," in *The Ministry in Historical Perspectives*, edited by H. Richard Niebuhr and Daniel Day Williams (N.Y.: Harper and Row, 1956).

Karl Rahner, "Priest and Poet," *Theological Investigations* 3 (Baltimore: Helicon, 1967).

----------, "The Point of Departure in Theology for Determining the Nature of the Priestly Office," *Theological Investigations* 12 (N.Y.: Seabury/Crossroad, 1974).

----------, "The Word and the Eucharist," *Theological Investigations* 4 (Baltimore: Helicon, 1966).

Joseph Ratzinger, *Theological Highlights of Vatican II* (N.Y.: Paulist, 1966).

----------, "Priestly Ministry: A Search for Its Meaning," *Emmanuel* 76 (1970): 442-53, 490-505.

----------, "Biblical Foundations of Priesthood," *Origins* 20 (October 18, 1990): 310-14.

----------, *Principles of Catholic Theology* (San Francisco: Ignatius, 1987).

Anthony Russell, *The Clerical Profession* (London: SPCK, 1980).

Edward Schillebeeckx, *Ministry: Leadership in the Community of Jesus Christ* (N.Y.: Crossroad, 1981).

98   John H. Morgan

----------, *The Church with a Human Face* (N.Y.: Crossroad, 1985).

Otto Semmelroth, "The Priestly People of God and Its Official Ministers," in *Concilium* 31, *The Sacraments in General* (N.Y.: Paulist Press, 1968).

Donald A. Schon, *Educating the Reflective Practitioner* (San Francisco: Jossey-Bass, 1987).

David S. Schuller, Milo L. Brekke, and Merton P. Strommen, *Ministry in America* (San Francisco: Harper & Row, 1980).

Donald M. Scott, *From Office to Profession* (Philadelphia: University of Pennsylvania Press, 1978).

John Shutz, *Paul and the Anatomy of Apostolic Authority* (Cambridge: Cambridge University Press, 1975).

Robert Sokolowski, *Eucharistic Presence: A Study in the Theology of Disclosure* (Washington, D.C.: Catholic University of America Press, 1994).

United States Bishops, "Go and Make Disciples: A National Plan and Stretegy for Catholic Evangelization in the United States," *Origins* 22 (December 3, 1992): 423-32.

IvanVallier, "Religious Specialists: Sociological Study," in *International Encyclopedia of the Social Sciences*, vol. 12, edited by David Sills, 444-453 (N.Y.: Crowell, Collier, and Macmillan, 1968).

Maurice Villain, "Can There Be Apostolic Succession Outside the Chain of Imposition of Hands?" *Concilium* 34, *Apostolic Succession: Rethinking a Barrier to Unity* (N.Y.: Paulist Press, 1968).

James D.Whitehead and Evelyn Eaton Whitehead, *Method in Ministry: Theological Reflection and Christian Ministry* (N.Y.: Seabury Press, 1981).

APPENDIX A

PHENOMENOLOGICAL SOCIOLOGY
as a Theoretical Infrastructure:
An Exploratory Prolegomenon to an Ecclesiastical Sociology

GENERAL INTRODUCTION

From the earliest records of human reflection, we learn that man has laboured
valiantly, fearlessly, and tirelessly to understand his world, his place in it, and
his relationship to it. The incomparable Greek philosopher, Aristotle,
expressed in his *Ethics* the unquestionable truth that all men seek to know.
Man, like all other animals, is equipped with sensory receptors and motor
effectors sufficient to respond to the demands of the physical world. But,
unlike other animals, man seems not driven merely to live a life of stimulus-
response, ever receiving signals and reacting accordingly. Man is unquestionably bent upon not only living life but grasping it, of owning it not simply as
provider of room and board but as a matrix within which his living has
meaning — value, purpose, duty.[1] Man's world is not strictly a physical
environment; rather, it is a symbolically endowed world of meanings, a world
that man not only encounters, but a world he seeks to understand. His world
is not so much a given as it is a discovery or a created panorama of interpret-
able symbols of meaning.[2] Man not only encounters, he interprets; he not only
responds, he discovers and creates as well. He seeks not merely to know the
world, but is driven to understand it and his relationship to it, to his fellow
men, and to himself. The more he encounters and is confronted by his
environment — physical, social, ideational — the more determined he is to
understand it and interpret its meaning. Truly it can be said that man is the
interpreting animal — *homo hermeneuticus.*[3]

To understand and to interpret the multidimensional world is man's chosen
vocation — a commitment made early when the cave man took up paints to
capture the mystery and the wonder of the hunt on the walls of his dwellings
and a commitment which still thrives in the medical laboratories and the halls
of the academy today. Man seeks to know and understand his world and
himself as he relates to it, and most recently, sociology as fledgling science has

joined in the great adventure of learning more about humankind. A youthful science in many respects, as compared to three thousand years of systematic philosophy and a half-millennium of astronomy, sociology has come along quickly in its own special parameters of research gaining acceptance and even respect from more established fields of learning. And like all other fields of research, as sociology has gained acceptance and flexed its scientific skills, it has produced sub-disciplines which claim specialized expertise in designated areas of the phenomena of social life. From an early sociology which aspired simply to study human social behaviour in interactional constellations of organizational settings, sociology has, in a brief period, given rise to specialized languages, research methodologies, and theoretical schools of thought which require advanced training and rigorous application in order to grasp their full interpretive potentials.

Within this framework has emerged phenomenological sociology and ethnomethodological sociology. Unlike the more traditional approaches in sociological theory and methodology which emphasize the historical and functional character of social behaviour, phenomenological sociology and ethnomethodological sociology are interpretive approaches to social life which emphasize 'the need to understand social action from the point of view of the social actor.'[4] In keeping with man's primordial urge to know and understand himself and his relationship to others, these two approaches attempt to identify (1) the meanings people find in their world — things, persons, events; (2) the perspectives from which people see themselves and others, and (3) the motives that underlie their behaviour. We might even suggest that these approaches exemplify the best motives and the most correct purpose for any social and behavioural science. 'Some have argued', say Chinoy and Hewitt, 'that this is the essential core of sociology.'[5]

If it is true that even original ideas have intellectual roots in the past reflections of thoughtful people, then it is fair to say that the ideational matrix within which phenomenological sociology and ethnomethodological sociology found roots and sprang to life is Husserlian philosophy and Mannheimian sociology. Though more will be said about both of these schools of thought later, a handy distinction is justified here between the traditional sociology of knowledge and phenomenological sociology as is practised today. The distinction is not so much a kind as it is an emphasis in analytical approaches and perspectives, for whereas 'phenomenological sociologists are interested in the foundations in intersubjective consciousness (individual's own personalistic reflections) of everyday life, the traditional sociology of knowledge has dealt with the relationship between socio-historical circumstances and knowledge, particularly intellectual knowledge.'[6] The most readily acclaimed expositor of the sociology of knowledge, Karl Mannheim, did not intend nor was he ever aware that from within his intellectual dominion two sub-disciplines were destined to spring—especially from his major work, *Ideology and Utopia* (1949),[7] providing the seedbed for further and divergent ideas. Mannheim drew heavily from his German countryman, Dilthey, whose philosophical writings in hermeneutics, i.e., the art of interpretation, produced in Mannheim the notion that knowledge is a product of one's own social and cultural setting. 'For Mannheim', wrote Sjoberg and Nett, 'knowledge is a product of one's social position, especially one's social class, within a society.'[8] Whereas Mannheim was almost exclusively interested in the socio-historical matrix of intellectual knowledge, later phenomenological and ethnomethodological sociologists turned their interest and attention to extremely subjectivistic, privatistic, and individualistic phenomena in the social arena.

A highly regarded extrapolation of Mannheim's early work coupled with phenomenological sensitivity to interpretation is found in Berger and Luckmann's work. 'Their basic assumption', explain Wallace and Wolf, 'is that everyday reality is a socially constructed system in which people give phenomena a certain order of reality... .'[9] Though Berger and Luckmann consider themselves revisionist sociologists of knowledge, their work is quite frequently cited as a good example of phenomenological sociology. They have explained rather carefully the duplicity of people's socially constructed reality — its objective as well as its subjective characteristics. With respect to the former, society, though admittedly a human product, is nevertheless and undeniably an objective reality which is another way of saying that society is external to the individual person who, in a real sense, is actually a product of society. However, as regards the subjective quality of reality socially constructed, Berger and Luckmann have written this: 'Everyday life presents itself as a reality interpreted by men and subjectively meaningful to them as a coherent world. Thus, society is actually constructed by activity that expresses meaning.'[10] Because both phenomenological and ethnomethodological sociologists are predicated on the 'point of view of the actor', it is easy to see how the sociology of knowledge, particularly as done by Berger and Luckmann, gets unsolicited credit for nurturing the rise of these two sub-disciplines. When in an earlier book, Berger says, 'Worlds are socially constructed and socially maintained',[11] he is articulating the perimeters of phenomenology and ethnomethodology; and when he goes on to say, 'their continuing reality, both objective (as common, taken-for-granted facticity) and subjective (as facticity imposing itself on individual consciousness), depends upon specific social processes, namely those processes that ongoingly reconstruct and maintain the particular worlds in question',[12] he corroborates their predisposition to study reality as interpreted by people in their everyday activities. Particularly, phenomenological sociology is sensitive to the inevitable threat to people these interpretations of social worlds cause, and the realization that a social base for continued interpretation is necessary for the sociologist himself is of special concern and interest to phenomenological sociologists. Within this context, we are later to discuss the practical as well as scientifically necessary employment of brackets around certain presumptions of phenomenologists and ethnomethodologists in order for them to be able to do their work.

Before we move on to a rather careful evaluation of each of the two sub-disciplines under discussion here, it might be helpful to compare and contrast briefly basic attitudes which characterize the phenomenologists' and the ethnomethodologists' perceptions of each other and their sociological colleagues outside their particular schools of thought and activity. Both for the traditional sociologist and the layman in the street, objects, events, and persons of the domain of everyday life are believed to exist independently of the mode of inquiry addressed to them — a simple philosophy of commonsense reality. For phenomenological and ethnomethodological sociologists, there is neither necessity nor justification for the constructing or the assuming of such a position about the 'real' world. Rather, for analytical purposes, what 'really' *is there* is irrelevant; but what *is thought to be there* by a social group is central. 'Both phenomenologists and ethnomethodologists', explains Heap and Roth, 'suspend or "bracket" the belief that such objects are independent of the mode of inquiry used to make the objects observable.'[13]   Therefore, instead of taking phenomena from the 'natural order' for analysis as do the socio-historical and functional schools of sociologists, the ethnomethodologists and the phenomenological sociologists hold in abeyance any truth-valid-real judgment about that order and concentrate their attention upon the 'real' world as it is thought, believed, and perceived to be by a social group. As Heap and Roth have carefully pointed out, another discernible difference between phenomenological and ethnomethodological sociology is their variant forms of reductionism. In the former, for instance, things in the 'real' world are *reduced* to things of immediate consciousness and are understood as being constituted 'in and through' intentional acts of consciousness. However, for ethnomethodology, the objectivized things of the social environment are *reduced* to the interpretational operations which assemble and reassemble 'things' for the ongoing constitution of the real world according to varying situations. Thus, conclude Heap and Roth, for phenomenological sociology, 'the foundational nexus of meaning' in man's world is that of 'immediate consciousness', whereas for ethnomethodology, 'the foundational nexus of meaning' is to be found in the 'immediately present, directly observed social situation' in the real world.[14] But, we should be quick to point out that anything which supposedly transcends this nexus (whether thought of as outside immediate consciousness or objects outside social situations) is bracketed, held in suspension, or 'put out of play' as relates to any analytical description or interpretation of the social world of human experience. The domain of phenomenological inquiry necessarily is limited to the analysis and interpretation of recognizable structures of immediate consciousness while the domain of ethnomethodological inquiry is focused specifically upon the limited perimeter of human activity which tends to construct, for the actors in the social matrix, a sense of objective realness about the world.

PHENOMENOLOGY

The term 'phenomenology' as it is used by Edmund Husserl (1859-1938) in his most notable philosophical treatise, *Ideas: Introduction to Pure Pheno- menology* (1913), designates first of all a principle of philosophical and scientific method. The usual method of natural science proceeds from a body of accepted truth and seeks to extend its conquest of the unknown by putting questions to nature and compelling it to answer. The phenomenological method adopts a softer approach. Setting aside all presuppositions and suppressing hypotheses (as far as humanly possible through rigorus self-examination), it seeks to devise techniques of observation, description, and classification which will permit it to disclose structures and connections in nature which do not yield to experimental techniques. *Ideas* was written with a view to clearing up the distinction between phenomenological psychology, which Husserl regarded as a legitimate, but secondary, science, and phenomenological philosophy, which, he was prepared to maintain, is the foundation of all science. When a sociologist or psychologist conducts a phenomenological investigation, he puts aside all the usual theories and assumptions which have governed research in that field; but he cannot rid himself of all presuppositions (such as, for example, the belief in the existence of the external world, the constancy of nature, etc.). As Plato saw, every science (except philosophy) must proceed upon some assumptions. To fulfill its promise, the phenomenological approach must bring us at last to an absolutely presuppositionless science. Pure phenomenology, or phenomenological philosophy, is, in Husserl's opinion, precisely that. (It has long been the aspiration of philosophers to make their science an absolute one, one that rids itself of all presuppositions and stands with open countenance before pure Being. Husserl stands in this tradition.)

Husserl pointed out that it seems innocent enough to explain consciousness in terms of natural courses until we recollect that matter and the laws which govern its behaviour are themselves part of our experience. This, according to Husserl, is the point at which the philosopher must step in. His primary task, in fact, will be to distinguish within experience the part that *experiences* from the part that is *experienced*. He talks, for example, of 'suspending' our natural beliefs, including the fundamental conviction of every healthy mind that there is a world 'out there', that there are other selves, and so on. We are asked to 'alter' this natural standpoint, to 'disconnect' our beliefs about causation and motion, to 'put them out of action'. This is, of course, only a methodological procedure, in order to help us overcome our animal bias and make it possible for us to take a coolly intellectual view of things. Greek philosophy used the term *epoche* to indicate the suspension of judgment. Husserl presses this term into his service.

As we shall immediately see, the phenomenological approach in sociology is based upon this particular philosophical foundation. Its beginnings can be detected in earlier periods of the discipline's development, but only in the third quarter of this century has it become a major theorectical and methodological school of thought gathering prominent and numerous followers and making grand efforts to contribute to the science. Husserl's phenomenology, as implied above, is as Timasheff suggested 'a critique of positivism or naturalistic empiricism which assumes that scientists through their five senses can investigate the world and build a body of knowledge that accurately reflects the objective reality of the world.'[15] This kind of naive empiricism is severely criticized by phenomenologists because it simplistically views the human mind as merely an empty container, or, as Edie has observed, the human mind is perceived to be nothing but 'the passive receptor of discreet, simple, atomic impressions from the 'outside world'.[16]

Husserl's phenomenology, then, was a major philosophical programme aimed at disclosing the absolute ground of human knowledge. His quest was based on a search for essences, which were seen as being unbound to the cultural or social sphere and thus not susceptible to the relativism and commonplace prejudices that characterize that realm. 'Husserl's fully developed philosophy', says Dickens, 'may be characterized as a philosophical hermeneutic aimed at disclosing the absolute grounds of human knowledge through a bringing to light of the unexpressed presuppositions which characterize that knowledge.'[17] Therefore, it is safe to say that, admittedly, the scientific status of phenomenologically informed inquiry is not based on the false guarantee of an absolute zero point as a starting point, but rather, it is the bringing to light of hidden biases and pretheoretical notions which constitute the objectivity of phenomenology-based inquiry. Because of the essentially historical nature of all understanding, the task of phenomenological clarification is always one of continuous criticism and reexamination. Husserl believed that a real and objective world exists, but because it is known only through subjective human consciousness, it is a socially constructed reality when it is interpreted. Phenomenology is considered a radical philosophical position which questions the empirical foundations of sociology as well as 'challenges the possibility of objective scientific knowledge, uninfluenced by the subjective consciousness of the investigator.'[18]

As we move from a brief, but hopefully informative exposure to pure phenomenology in the domain of philosophy to that of applied phenomenology in the domain of sociology, we must remember that phenomenological sociology must be regarded as the antithesis of neopositivism. As noted above, the development of phenomenological sociology questions the empirical foundations of sociology, thereby challenging the adequacy and meaningfulness of traditional sociological knowledge. If phenomenological sociology is to have any claim to a distinctive perspective and any relationship to Husserl's phenomenology, Timasheff says that 'it must focus on the analysis of the structure of consciousness and relationship of the consciousness of the individual to the social fabric.'[19]

It should be emphasized at this point that Husserl actually knew little of the concrete or conceptual problems of the social and behavioural sciences. Yet, even though there is strong sentiment in certain philosophical, as well as sociological circles, that phenomenological sociology is simply not possible, there is a vocal, literate, and growing body of sociologists who are setting about the development of just this kind of approach, building primarily on the work of the German expatriate Alfred Schutz who is considered more or less the founder of phenomenological sociology, or at least responsible for the introduction and development of the sub-discipline on American soil. In his work, he attempted to clarify Max Weber's concept of 'action' and his method of 'ideal type' construction. Schutz, explain Heap and Roth, 'revealed the invariant formal structures of the life-world — the realms of manipulation and the system of relevance and typification.'[20] Before we discuss Schutz's contributions, it should be pointed out that early philosophically-inclined sociologists in Europe had already begun to explore some of the issues addressed in phenomenology, particularly the German sociologist Alfred Vierkandt (1867-1952), and the Frenchman Jules Monnerot of the same period. Vierkandt, whose books include *Natural and Cultural People* (1895), and *Theory of Society* (1922), believed that society is the sum total of human interaction (not a novel idea to be sure) and his method, called 'ideational abstraction', consisted of a quest 'for basic unreducible concepts clarified through contemplation'. This emphasis on the 'irreducible' and 'contemplation' plays heavily in Schutz's work. Monnerot, author of *Social Facts Are Not Things* (1946), was rabidly anti-Durkheimian as suggested in the title of his book. His work consisted of a study of social situations which precipitate immediate experiences analysable by sociology — a sociology built upon the conviction that 'social facts', as Durkheim called social phenomena, are really just humanly defined and perceived 'conditions' or situations, thus factual only in the sense that humanly contrivances might be considered facts.

Alfred Schutz (1899-1959) was a social philosopher who fled Germany in 1939 to escape the Nazis. Gifted and talented in banking and ingenuity, Schutz took a daytime position in a New York City bank to support himself and taught social philosophy classes in the evening at the New School for Social Research in 1943. Nine years later, he became professor of sociology and philosophy and continued to teach at the New School until his death in 1959. Schutz is generally credited with introducing phenomenology to American sociology.   He assigned central importance to the meaning individuals impart to situations in everyday life and adapted Husserl's philosophy to sociology, as well as incorporated Weber's concept of *verstehen,* or subjective understanding, into his system.   In his attempt to apply Husserl's phenomenological philosophy to social science problems, Schutz found that Weber's concept of *verstehen* fitted nicely with his own emphasis upon individual consciousness.   Schutz fundamentally believed that the 'experience and assumption of shared meanings built the foundation which made social life possible.'

The main source of Schutz's writings for a careful and systematic presentation of his system is *The Phenomenology of the Social World,* (first published in 1932 but recently reprinted by Northwestern University Press in 1967).   His papers and lectures have recently been combined into three *Collected Papers*: Volume One. *The Problem of Social Reality* (1962); Volume Two, *Studies in Social Theory* (1964); and Volume Three, *Studies in Phenomenological Philosophy* 1966), all published by Martinus Mijhoff in The Hague.   Two major elements in social relations which became the focus of Schutz's analysis are what he labeled 'uniqueness and typification'.   All repetitive social situations constitute a process called typification-categorizing of situations and persons into types based on socially shared definitions and meanings.   In face-to-face relations, typification is necessarily modified by unique situations.   Thus, the rule of thumb is that the more personal the relationship, the more unique its character is bound to be; and the more impersonal the relationship, the more typified.   For a critical discussion of this facet of Schutz's work, see Helmut R. Wagner's edited volume, entitled *Alfred Schutz on Phenomenology and Social Relations* (1970).   For Schutz, the meaning that the individual imparts to situations in everyday life is of prime importance; he puts the spotlight on the individual's own definition of the situation.   And he believes that the meaning an individual imparts to the interaction situation may be shared by the person with whom he is interacting; Schutz calls this 'reciprocity of perspectives'.   An example Wallace and Wolf use to explain the idea is that of members in an orchestra.   Because the musicians in an orchestra share their meanings of the situation with the conductor, the musicians could exchange positions with the conductor and experience the situation the way the conductor does.   'Shared meaning', Wallace and Wolf explain,[21] 'may be assumed and experienced in the interaction situation.   In such situations, people are acting on the basis of taken-for-granted assumptions about reality.' Husserl spoke, in his system, of an 'ontology of the life-world', meaning, we assume, that *a priori* framework of the humanly experienced environment within which man lives his life. Schutz, not wishing merely to reiterate this philosophical postulate, 'sought to elucidate the *a priori* structure of the world in which sociological phenomena are apprehended.'[22] Therefore, we can assume that rather than seeking the 'essence' of, say, corporations or the state or religion, Schutz would rather turn to the structures of the life-world which those entities presuppose, such as a world of contemporaries beyond our reach grasped through socially distributed and pragmatically generated typifications. For Schutz, these structures inherent in social phenomena, i.e., *a priori* 'ontological' givens, included intersubjectivity, of which he began but never completed, an interpretation through a kind of scientific methodology he called the 'constitutive phenomenology of the natural attitude'. This natural attitude, which intrigued him so much, is defined as that attitude of naive belief in the existence of the world as perceived and really believed to be 'out there'. 'Life-world', 'intersubjectivity', and the 'natural attitude' are the tripartite pillars of Schutz's theory of phenomenological sociology, and claim Heap and Roth, 'the type of sociology founded on Schutz's phenomenology is constituted most notably by Berger and Luckmann'.[23]

Before further consideration can be given to Berger and Luckmann, who incidentally consider themselves phenomenological sociologists of knowledge, some attention must be focused upon Karl Mannheim who is to the sociology of knowledge what Schutz is to phenomenological sociology, and, as with the latter, so with the former, Edmund Husserl's philosophical system proved determinative in the development of their various schools of thought. Karl Mannheim (1893-1947), a German sociologist, was born in Budapest and died in London. He studied at Berlin and Paris, and at Heidelberg under Max Weber. His thought resembles that of such philosophers as Comte and Hegel, who believed that in the past man had been dominated by the historical process, whereas in the future he would gain ascendency over it. In his first and most important book, *Ideology and Utopia* (1936), Mannheim asserted that the act of cognition must not be regarded as the effort of a purely theoretical consciousness, because the human consciousness is permeated by nontheoretical elements arising both from man's participation in social life and in the streams and tendencies of willing, which work themselves out contemporaneously in that life. Mannheim, therefore, argued for a new discipline to address this new level of understanding and analysing man's own knowledge, viz., the sociology of knowledge. According to Mannheim, this new discipline revealed that all knowledge, or at least knowledge of things human, was situation-bound (*situationsgebunden*) — that is, tied to a given constellation of socio-historical circumstances. Each age develops its own style of thought, and comparisons between these styles are impossible, since each posits a different basic sphere. Even within each age there are conflicting tendencies toward conservation, on the one hand, and toward change on the other. Commitment to conservation tends to produce 'ideologies' — to falsify thought by excessive idealization of the past and overemphasis on the factors making for stability. Intentness on change is apt to produce 'utopias', which overvalue both the future and factors leading to change.

Mannheim suggested, by way of anticipating the later sociologists of knowledge such as Berger and Luckmann, that between ideology and utopia there is at least the possibility of completely realistic (*situationsgerecht*) thought that functions without friction within the given framework of life, and is set neither on pushing forward nor on holding back the development of society. But Mannheim places little emphasis on this possibility. He sees a very strong tendency toward the polarization of society into hostile camps. Only the comparatively uncommitted intelligentsia is likely to approach nearer the truth. From its special and particularly favourable vantage point, it could, and should, elaborate a 'total perspective' which would synthesize the conflicting contemporary world views and thereby neutralize, and to some extent overcome, their onesidedness. Such a 'dynamic synthesis', Mannheim thought, is the nearest possible approximation to a truly realistic attitude, within the limitations imposed upon a given epoch. He held, therefore, that every socio-historical situation is located at a specific point along a unilinear, ever-progressing and never-returning temporal continuum — history. Each situation is, therefore, unique, and the knowledge to which it gives birth, and which is true within it, is equally unique, bound to its time and place, and relative.

However, Mannheim, as the father of the sociology of knowledge, was not primarily concerned with the truth of propositions. Rather, he operated with a radically different conception of 'truth'. To him, truth is an attribute, not so much of discourse, as of reality. The individual who is in contact with the living forces of his age has the truth, or better, is in the truth — a conception which shows at once Mannheim's Marxism, his historicism, and his pragmatism. He was moving close to the belief that the traditional correspondence of thought-and-reality should be replaced by a correspondence of thought-and-situation. Mannheim, in short, was interested in the genuineness, rather than in the truth *per se*, of a given world view.

As we have seen, Mannheim owes much to Husserl's phenomenology. Coser has pointed out that 'what impressed Mannheim in Husserl's phenomenology was not the attempt to penetrate to knowledge of pure essences...but rather Husserl's emphasis on the "intentionality" of human thought.'[24] Husserl, as we noted earlier, has contended that the sharp separation between knower and known and the essentially passive conception of the act of knowing in most modern philosophy had to be abandoned in favour of an activist conception of knowledge through 'intentional' activity. Peter Berger and Thomas Luckmann's leading work in the phenomenological sociology of knowledge is their book, entitled, *The Social Construction of Reality* (1967). They are quick to point out their distinction from a more traditional sociology of knowledge, says Timasheff, because their emphasis has not been particularly concerned, as is the traditional sociology of knowledge, 'with epistemological questions about the validity of knowledge (e.e., the extent to which ideas or what people think they know are shaped by social and historical circumstances) and with the history of ideas.'[25]

Though Berger and Luckmann are more or less unconcerned with questions of the ultimate validity of knowledge *per se*, they are rather profoundly concentrated in their work upon the question of how whatever is accepted as knowledge in a society has come to be accepted as such. In other words, they are primarily concerned with 'the processes by which *any* body of "knowledge" comes to be socially established as "reality." ' In their own writings, they have contended that the sociology of knowledge is concerned with the analysis of the social construction of reality. Thus, having departed from the traditional empirical foundation of scientific sociology, the phenomenologically oriented sociologists — under the various, but ever present influence of Husserl — hold the reality of the social world in abeyance, preferring to focus not upon 'social facts', so-called, but upon the structure of intersubjective consciousness and the creation of social meaning in human interaction. In a differentiated branch of phenomenological sociology, known as ethnomethodology, as we shall see later, concern is centered on the process by which commonsense reality is constructed in everyday face-to-face interaction.

Several concepts which, though not unique to Schutz and phenomenological sociology, have received special consideration and sometimes unique interpretations and usage should, for a moment, capture our attention. The meaning and use of the concept of 'reduction', though already mentioned earlier, deserves a further hearing because of its central place in Schutz's understanding of what phenomenological sociology is all about. 'The phenomenologist', he writes in 1962, 'does not deny the existence of the outer world, but for his analytical purpose he makes up his mind to suspend belief in its existence — that is, to refrain intentionally and systematically from all judgements related directly or indirectly to the existence of the outer world.'²⁶ This bracketing or suspending of judgement or holding in abeyance as best one can predispositions of interpretation, in some ways is the core of phenomenological sociology. 'What we have put into brackets', Schutz goes on to say, 'is not only the existence of outer world, along with all the things in it, inanimate and animate, including fellow-men, cultural objects, society and its institutions...but also the propositions of all sciences.'²⁷

One of Schutz's and later phenomenological sociologists' problematical terms employed readily in philosophical phenomenology is the concept of 'essence', a term of questionable utility for the sociologist and one that requires definition. Heap and Roth, more so than any others since Schutz, have offered specific help in this matter. 'Essence', they write, 'may be taken to be that intuited invariant quality without which the intended object, the phenomenon, would not be what it is....Essence has as its reference the *a priori* realm of possibilities which precedes that of actualities.'²⁸ Therefore, say the phenomenologists, essence is 'intuited' from the intended object — object as 'experienced', as 'perceived'. Schutz has explained that essence is 'arrived at' through the method of 'reduction' and 'imaginative variation'. An object's defining or distinguishing qualities and characteristics are arrived at *a posteriori*, through logical operations based on factual knowledge about actual objects in the taken-to-be-real world.

Another highly problematical, but potentially useful concept for phenomenological sociologists discussed by Heap and Roth, is 'phenomenon'. Present-day sociologists employing phenomenological language and method seem drawn to Husserl's dictum — 'to the things themselves' — which seems to mean a return to the phenomena-as-given in the immediate consciousness. 'By phenomenon', explain Heap and Roth, 'Husserl meant that which, having been subjected to the phenomenological reduction, is purified from the reality attributed to it by "naive consciousness".'[29] A phenomenon as such only becomes available when we cease to treat an object as real, and begin to treat the object as meant, as intended, as it appears. Mention here of 'intend' calls to mind the role 'intentionality' played in Husserl's formal language and methodology. Though it is true that intentionality can be equated with 'purpose', it is so only at the predictive level of experience, that is, the level of judgment, or of 'action', in Weber's sense. 'However', Heap and Roth explain, 'Husserl's theory of intentionality refers also to the pre-predicative level. This is the level of immediate experience, of perception, of so-called non-meaningful behaviour, in Weber's sense.'[30]

When a phenomenological sociologist uses terms such as 'reality', 'subjective', and 'objective', the uninitiated should be careful in not assuming a particular taken-for-granted meaning. These terms for phenomenologists become specialized nomenclature in the sociological laboratory. Subjective reality, Timasheff has explained, means 'an individual's acceptance of a set of beliefs, expectations, definitions, meanings, and evaluations as his or her own view of the world which develops through the process of socialization', whereas 'Objective reality is socially shared reality; when meanings are shared by a group, they become objectified by virtue of being external to the individual persons who share common typification, i.e., common evaluations about types of persons and situations and the behaviour appropriate to them, share a common social world.'[31]

Thus, we can see that a social structure is the sum total of these typifications and of the recurrent patterns of interaction established by means of them. Finally, and in keeping with the specialized definitions of common sociological terms, we are able to define 'institution' in a phenomenologically correct fashion, by saying that institution is a 'set of patterned (habitualized) reciprocal typifications.'[32] The individual experiences the institutional world as an objective reality, but the apparently objective world is really a humanly constructed objectivity. A reflective consciousness, however, is able to superimpose the quality of logic upon the institutional order. And 'the logic by which the institutions of society are integrated is known as *legitimation*, which interrelates more limited meanings embodied in specific institutions by means of broader schemes of meaning.'[33] Thus, in keeping with the phenomenological spirit of Schutz's sociology, it can be said that all symbolic universes and all legitimations are human products; their existence has its reality or validity in the lives of concrete individuals, and has no empirical status apart from these lives.

Schutz specifically and phenomenological sociology generally have not gone without criticism — some severe and unjust, some productive and insightful. A strong critique of a single deductive model for the form of a theory, such as expounded in this school of thought, comes from Maurice Natanson, an existential and phenomenological philosopher and sound student of the social and behavioural sciences. In his critiques and formal writings, he has called upon social scientists to be more self-critical, more theorectical, and certainly more philosophically literate in their conception of theory and theory-construction, calling upon them to examine more internally critically the 'worldview' underlying their own arguments about theory and methodology. Warshy has provided an excellent example of both pro and con deductive models: '...tending toward the deductive model', he explains, 'is an "objective" worldview that, following a materialistic conception of consciousness, places the individual in the context of all natural phenomena,' yet, he counters, 'tending away from the deductive model, and from modern science as usually understood, is a "subjective" worldview that, following a phenomenological approach to social reality, sees natural science as but one aspect of the intersubjective world produced by the activity of consciousness.'[34] In spite of Natanson's criticisms of phenomenological sociology, he has made significant contributions to its development and integrity in the scientific and philosophical communities, especially in his edited volume entitled, *Philosophy of the Social Sciences* (1963). For instance, Natanson has employed the concepts of social role and typification to analyse 'intersubjective consciousness' — Schutz's term. Individuals internalize conceptions of social toles involving typification, i.e., socially shared expectations and evaluations of behaviour in particular situations, which include 'self-typifications', that is, images and evaluations of the roles one personally plays as well as role typifications of others. Natanson has used extensively these concepts not only to analyse 'sociality', a major concern of his, but also the relation of persons to science, art, and religion. And as it stands now, Natanson's constructive criticism of phenomenological sociology's weaknesses and his effective utilization of its strengths has served well the further development of one of American sociology's most provocative and challenging theoretical constructs and methodological programs since the appearance of symbolic interaction.

ETHNOMETHODOLOGY

Growing out of the general developments of sociology of knowledge came a widespread legitimization of fundamental questions about the traditional discipline's presupposition about its subject matter, its view of the world, and cognitive processes operative in human behaviour. For example, how do sociologists and other groups of human create and sustain for each other the presumption that the social world has a real character? And, as a result of posing such a question, a more 'real' phenomenon revolves around the complex ways people go about consciously and unconsciously constructing, maintaining, and altering their sense of an external social reality. 'In fact,' Turner has pointed out in some detail, 'the cement that holds society together may not be the values, norms, common definitions, exchange payoffs, role bargains, interest coalitions, and the like of current social theory', rather he argues convincingly that it may be 'people's explicit and implicit "methods" for creating the presumption of a social order.'[35] These comments, of course, lead us directly to a consideration of ethnomethodology which, as Zimmerman is quick to point out, 'is not a comprehensive theory of society...(but rather) is an approach to the study of the fundamental bases of social order.'[36] Ethnomethodology concerns itself primarily with those structures of social interaction which would be invariant to the revolutionary transformation of a society's institutions. As a perspective, and as yet hardly claiming to be a 'subdiscipline', ethnomethodology has not concerned itself with such issues as power, the distribution of resources in society, or the historical shape of institutions.

Phenomenological sociologists understand the task of sociology fundamentally as describing precisely how we see the world, and although they emphasize that our perceptions are molded intrinsically by our concepts, the phenomeno-logical sociologists are not recognizably different from the sociologists of knowledge. The difference in emphasis, not in kind, seems to accentuate the domain of the ethnomethodologists. They all examine the ways we come to have similar perceptions to those of others — how we put together the phenomena we experience in such a way that we all construct a similar or shared 'everyday world.' Though ethnomethodologists really acknowledge their indebtedness to both phenomenological and the sociology of knowledge traditions, they are equally quick to emphasize their distinctive perspective.

The work of such sociologists as Schutz, Berger, and Luckmann is primarily philosophical and macroscopic, stressing the primacy of studying the processes of human consciousness, and concerned with the general nature of realities. The ethnomethodologists, on the other hand, have extended the concerns of symbolic interactionism and phenomenology, and focus on microscopic aspects of human behaviour. They are especially interested in the empirical analysis of the ways in which particular meanings are constructed. Yet, it must be noted that in the area of small group (micro) versus large group (macro) sociology, many sociologists, particularly ethnomethodologists, involved in micro-sociology do not accept the rationale for a separate theory of micro and macro analysis. The ethnomethodologists unreservedly acclaim the exclusive validity of micro approaches and contend that larger social structures can be meaningfully understood only by studying small groups and other face-to-face situations. For ethnomethodologists, the theoretical concern centres around the processes by which commonsense reality is constructed in everyday face-to-face interaction. With this focus, it is plain to see that ethnomethodology can quite rightly be judged a distinctive branch of phenomenological sociology, which, in common with other phenomenological forms in the United States, derived in large part from the work of Alfred Schutz, as discussed above. It is obvious that Schutz strongly influenced Harold Garfinkel, the founder of ethnomethodology, who sought to understand the methods employed by people to make sense out of their world.

However, before we take a closer look at Garfinkel's work, an overview of ethnomethodology seems in order. This approach to sociology studies the process by which people invoke certain taken-for-granted rules about behaviour with which they interpret an interaction situation and make it meaningful. 'To ethnomethodology', explain Wallace and Wolf, 'the interpretive process is a phenomenon for investigation.' They point out that 'ethomethodology does not aim to "explain" human behaviour or to show why, for example, places and generations vary in their suicide and divorce rates, or why religion "really" exists.'[38] The emphasis, rather, in this perspective is on description (reflecting affinities with phenomenology), and the subject matter — people's methods of making sense of their social world — poses different questions from those asked by traditional sociology. Ethnomethodologists are, therefore, interested in the interpretations people use to make sense of social settings.

As we have seen, Harold Garfinkel is the recognized founder of ethnomethodology. Born in 1917, Garfinkel completed his Ph.D. (Harvard) in 1952, and aside from a couple of brief teaching stints at Ohio State and the University of Chicago, he has taught since 1954 at the University of California at Los Angeles. To date, he has published no single major work, but has had many of his best articles published in a collected volume, entitled, *Studies in Ethnomethodology*, by Prentice-Hall in 1967. Garfinkel's work differs considerably from Durkheim's over the issue of 'social facts'. Garfinkel saying no and Durkheim saying yes to their *sui generis* objective reality. Ethnomethodology, rather, sees the objective reality of social facts, says Garfinkel, as an 'ongoing accomplishment of the concerted activities of everyday life.'[39] Much of the distinction in perspective between traditional sociology and ethnomethodology can be established in the definition of the latter term. The term's meaning can be understood in terms of a form of folk technique by which actors in social interaction 'think up' a series of accounts or verbal description that enable them to construct social reality as they perceive it. Ethnomethodologists, on the other hand, are interested in the ways in which people create a sense of reality. By 'making sense' of events in terms of preconceived order for society, people create a world that is indeed ordered.

The term 'ethnomethodology' itself was coined while Garfinkel was working at Yale with their cross-cultural files. During this time he was working on an analysis of jury tape-recordings when he came upon the file card categories of 'ethnobotany', 'ethnophysiology', 'ethnophysics', etc. He became extremely interested in how the jurors knew what they were doing in doing the work of jurors. In such things as the juror's use of some kind of knowledge of the way in which the organized affairs of the society operated, it occurred to him that on the jury deliberation project that he was faced with jurors who were actually doing methodology. 'He created "ethnomethodology",' explains Roy Turner, 'because "ethno" refers to the availability to a member of common-sense knowledge of his society as commonsense knowledge of the "whatever".'[40] Thus ethnomethodology is the study of 'folk' or commonsense methods employed by people to make sense of everyday activities by constructing and maintaining social reality.

Ethnomethodologists do not use a commonsense method, rather, they study commonsense methods of constructing reality. They use, explains Timasheff, the 'phenomenological frame-work' which is in essence the antithesis of the everyday commonsense interpretation of social life. The term itself, adds Mullins, was coined by Harold Garfinkel 'to reflect his belief that the proper subject for social science is the way in which ordinary people establish rational behaviour patterns.'[41] Ordinary people use various methods to determine what is happening in society; 'this methodology', continues Mullins, 'is "ethno" in that, like "ethnobotany", it is derived from folk knowledge rather than from professional scientific procedures.'[42] Hence, ethnomethodology is the study of the methods used by members of a group for understanding community, making decisions, being rational, accounting for action, and so on.

Garfinkel has proposed the idea of an emergent, negotiable, shifting order in his ethnomethodological programme, emphasizing the vast web of common-sense understandings and folk classifications that all members of common-place organized social situations take for granted — these are still in flux. There persists a preference for qualitative techniques in field research over the merely quantitative. Garfinkel stresses, Warshay points out, 'the common understandings underlying simple daily social conversations and transactions.' Ethnomethodologists, he continues, 'study both biography and purpose of actors as well as analysis of the commonsense understandings of ordinary social life.'[43] It must occasionally be pointed out that, strictly speaking, ethnomethodology is not a new research method. It does not, for instance, seek to answer the question of how society is possible by introducing sociologists to new research techniques. Rather, explains Jonathan Turner, 'ethnomethodology is concerned with the study of a phenomenon that has received little attention within the intellectual confines of traditional theoretical perspectives. It seeks to study, Turner explains, 'this phenomenon by the use of many research strategies, including variants of observational and participant-observational methods.'[44] Garfinkel wrote a short paper, later included in Roy Turner's edited volume, Ethnomethodology, entitled, 'The Origins of the Term "Ethnomethodology"', in which the personal as well as the intellectual dimensions of the term's emergence are recounted.[45] Seldom are details such as these available to give posterity an exact account of a theoretical term's birth. Earlier, we saw how Husserl's work called for 'bracketing' or holding in abeyance the external world, *per se,* while studying 'pure consciousness'. But, with ethnomethodology, there is a specific bracketing of the social order while studying intersubjective consciousness in the interactive situation. Instead of studying the social order, *per se,* or empirically ascertaining objective reality, ethnomethodology seeks to understand how people in interaction create and maintain a conception of social reality. According to ethnomethodologists, what is most readily observable, and hence real, are the attempts by interacting humans to persuade each other that there is an order to specific social settings and to a broader society. 'What is "really real"', then, explains Turner, 'are the methods people employ in constructing, maintaining, and altering for each other a sense of order — regardless of the content and substance of their formulations.'[46]

The sense of order is not what makes society possible, say the ethnomethodologists, but rather the capacity of humans to actively and continually create and use rules for persuading each other that there is a real world. They place much emphasis upon the necessity for understanding any situation from the point of view of the actors or interactional participants. 'Since meaning is seen as created in the process of interaction', explains Timasheff, 'its only reality is the interpretation given to it by the person involved in the interactive process, and this is what the investigator must seek to understand.'[47] As we have already seen, the ethnomethodologist is primarily interested in the world as perceived by people and as interpreted by them within social networks. The 'perceiving' component of this dual emphasis suggests affinities with phenomenological sociology, as we have seen already, and the latter is more suggestive of ethnomethodology's allegiance to the sociology of knowledge school. George Psathas has, in a rather fine way, articulated the nature and complexity of the relationship between these two fledgling schools in his essay entitled 'Ethnomethodology and Phenomenology.' For ethnomethodologists, what is directly observable are people's efforts to create a commonsense of social reality, and, explains Jonathan Turner, 'the substance of this reality is viewed as less interesting than the methods used by groups of people to construct, reaffirm, and alter a vision and image of what exists "out there".'[48]

Though ethnomethodology has not as yet refined or even identified its most effective analytical techniques, there are four more or less regularly employed methods evident in the work of most ethnomethodologists. Besides the tradition of participant-observation (well used in cultural anthropology and symbolic interaction), there is what is called the 'ethnomethodological experiment' which essentially calls for a disrupting of any interactive situation by acting (on the part, usually, of the researcher or one in his charge) incongruous with the situation's norms. 'Documentary interpretation,' a third method, consists of taking behaviour, statements, etc., and other external appearances of the other (any other person or group) as a 'document' or reflection of an underlying pattern used to interpret appearances. And finally, a significant interest exists in linguistics as *communication of meaning*, with special attention placed upon the relationship between linguistic *form* and the *structure* of social interaction. The overlapping in methodological presuppositions and processes between ethnomethodology and phenomenology is reflected, as we said, in George Psathas' paper, and another comparative study appropriate to these methodological considerations is Norman K. Denzin's study of the similarities and dissimilarities between ethnomethodology and symbolic interaction, most recently discussed by him in his paper entitled, 'Symbolic Interaction and Ethnomethodology: A Proposed Synthesis.' To the ethnomethodologist, symbols and meanings have no existence apart from their interpretation by persons in interaction. Ethnomethodology avoids the whole question of reality (a pitfall, as these practitioners see it, in virtually all traditional sociology), choosing rather to emphasize the study of the ways an image of social reality is created. 'Because they have rejected the basic assumption of empirical sociology,' says Timasheff, namely, that there is a real social and cultural world capable of being objectively studied by scientific methods, 'ethnomethodologists regard their approach as a radical break with all branches of traditional sociology and not merely another conceptual framework.'[49] One of the particularly problematical factors in their methodological process is their emphasis upon the uniqueness of each and every interactive situation and their suspicions about all generalizable similarities between interactive situations. Ethnomethodologists are interested in situations as 'creations' by participants who are viewed as having much freedom to alter, reinterpret, and change their social environment by acts of will.

Of course, their dubious feelings about all generalizations upon human behaviour are demonstrative of their ideological rejection of all metaphysical assumptions made by traditional empirical sociology.[50] The ethnomethodologist challenges traditional sociology's assumption that there is a sufficiently stable system of shared meanings in a society to provide a basis for meaningful responses to questionnaires or interviews or any type of research method in which the researcher fits subjects' responses or behaviour into predetermined categories. Wallace and Wolf, in their sympathetic defense of ethnomethodology have paid special attention to a concept employed in this kind of social analysis, called 'accounting,' which, in some ways at least, allows the perspective its skepticism about generalizations while not paralyzing its analytical interests. 'Accounting,' they explain, 'is people's ability to announce to themselves and others the meaning they are getting out of a situation.' 'Accounts,' they explain, 'involve both language and meaning; people are constantly giving linguistic or verbal accounts as they explain their actions.'[51] Garfinkel, for instance, has urged ethnomethodologists to call attention to reflexive practices, such as, when a child is asked to 'tell about' his or her own creative production and then proceeds to do so and to interpret the figures, shapes, and colours in the drawing to another person, the child is giving an 'account.' This technique, along with others mentioned earlier, has provided ethnomethodologists with the kind of practical research tools and topics which promise to advance the discipline through research and publication.

As might be suspected, the reaction of many sociologist has been to ignore, or misunderstand, or criticize, or in some happy cases integrate it into their own conventional approaches. Of course, as we have seen, a major criticism is ethnomethodology's neglect of what Berger and Luckmann call the objectification of social reality — a serious criticism by any standard, and one with which the discipline must come to grips. And finally, from the macrosociologists, their rather formidable criticism is of ethnomethodologists' bracketing of the social order, with major emphasis upon the interpretative situation, which precludes any adequate account being taken of such large systems as power or class structure. Needless to say, the ethnomethodologists have much work yet to do in the particular areas of criticism before they can become full participants in sociological research alongside traditional sociology.

NOTES

1. For a critical study of the literature on the crisis of meaning in contemporary society, see John H. Morgan, *In Search of Meaning: From Freud to Teilhard de Chardin* (Washington D.C., The University Press of America, 1977).

2. For a careful analysis of the concept of 'culture' in terms of its 'meaning-bearing qualities' as interpreted by symbolic anthropology, see John H. Morgan, 'Religion and Culture as Meaning Systems,' *The Journal of Religion*, LVII, 4 (October, 1977), 363, 375.

3. A thorough investigation of the concept of man as an essentially interpretive animal is to be found in John H. Morgan (ed.), *Understanding Religion and Culture* (Washington D.C., The University Press of America, 1979).

4. Ely Chinoy and John P. Hewitt, *Sociological Perspective* (New York, Random House, 1975), p. 156.

5. Ibid.

6. Nicholas S. Timasheff and George Theodorson, *Sociological Theory* (New York, Random House, 1967), p. 352.

7. Karl Mannheim, *Ideology and Utopia* (New York, Harcourt, Brace, and World, 1949).

8. Gideon Sjoberg and Roger Nett, *A Methodology for Social Research* (New York, Harper and Row, 1968).

9. Ruth Wallace and Alison Wolf, *Contemporary Sociological Theory* (Englewood Cliffs, Prentice-Hall, 1980), p. 266.

10. Peter Berger and Thomas Luckmann, *The Social Construction of Reality* (New York, Doubleday, 1966), p. 19.

122   John H. Morgan

11.   Peter L. Berger, *The Sacred Canopy* (New York, Doubleday, 1969), p. 45.

12.   Ibid.

13.   James Heap and Phillip Roth, 'On Phenomenological Society,' *American Sociological Review*, 38 (June 1973), 288.

14.   Ibid.

15.   Timasheff and Theodorson, op. Cit., 291.

16.   James Edie, *What is Phenomenology?* (Chicago, Quandrangle Books, 1962), p. 19.

17.   David Dickens, 'Phenomenology,' in Scott McNall (ed.) *Theoretical Perspectives in Sociology* (New York, St. Martin's Press, 1979), p. 345.

18.   See Timasheff and Theodorson, *Sociological Theory*, pp. 291-305. Also, for an informative discussion of Husserl's phenomenology with a sociological sensitivity, cf. Maurice Natanson, *Edmund Husserl Philosopher of Infinite Tasks* (Evanston, Northwestern University Press, 1973).

19.   Timasheff and Theodorson, op. Cit., p. 298.

20.   Heap and Roth, op. Cit., p. 287.

21.   Wallace and Wolf, op. Cit., p. 265.

22.   Heap and Roth, op. Cit., p. 287.

23.   Ibid.

24.   Lewis Coser, *Masters of Sociological Thought* (New York, Free Press, 1971), p. 454.

25.   Timasheff and Theodorson, op. Cit., p. 298.

26. Alfred Schutz, *The Problem of Social Reality*, Volume 1 (The Hague, Martinus Mijhoff, 1962), p. 104.

27. Ibid., p. 105.

28. Heap and Roth, op. Cit., p. 283.

29. Ibid., p. 281.

30. Ibid., p. 280.

31. Timasheff and Theodorson, op. Cit., p. 299.

32. Ibid.

33. Ibid.

34. Leon H. Warshay, *The Current State of Sociological Theory* (New York, David McKay, 1975), p. 112.

35. Jonathan Turner, *The Structure of Sociological Theory* (Homewood, The Dorsey Press, 1974), p. 321.

36. Don H. Zimmerman, 'Ethnomethodology,' *'The American Sociologist,'* 13 (February, 1978), 6-15.

37. The diversity of phenomenological sociology in the United States is brought out in the collection of essays edited by George Psathas, *Phenomenological Sociology: Issues and Applications* (New York, Wiley, 1973).

38. Wallace and Wolf, op. Cit., p. 270.

39. Harold Garfinkel, *Studies in Ethnomethodology* (Englewood Cliffs, Prentice Hall, 1967), p. vii.

40.   H. R. Wagner (ed.), *Alfred Schutz on Phenomenology and Social Relations* (Chicago, The University of Chicago Press, 1970), p. 16.

41.   Nicholas C. Mullins, *Theories and Theory Groups in Contemporary American Sociology* (New York, Harper and Row, 1973), p. 184.

42.   Ibid.

43.   Warshay, op. Cit., p. 37.

44.   J. Turner, op. Cit., p. 324.

45.   R. Turner, *Ethnomethodology* (Balt, Penguin Books, 1974), pp. 16-17.

46.   J. Turner, op. Cit., p. 330.

47.   Timasheff and Theodorson, op. Cit., p. 302.

48.   J. Turner, op. Cit., p. 322.

49.   Timasheff and Theodorson, op. Cit., p. 301.

50.   For a careful critique of this position, see Aaron V. Cicourel, *Method and Measurement in Sociology* (New York, Free Press, 1964).

51.   Wallace and Wolf, op. Cit., p. 272.

APPENDIX B

PASTORAL ECSTASY AND THE AUTHENTIC SELF:
Theological Meanings in Symbolic Distance

Of all the descriptive terms that flash through our minds when thinking of the plight of the reverend clergy, *ecstasy* is probably the last to appear, *frustration, confusion,* and *bewilderment,* or more generous terms like *nice, pleasant,* and *easygoing* are, of course, the more generally expected and accepted descriptions of pastors. If, however, we are called upon to characterize the creative mood of poets, artists, writers, and, indeed, mystics and holy persons, ecstasy comes readily to mind. And yet, if there is a vocation, a calling in the true sense of that concept, in need of the transcendent experience of ecstasy, we would probably feel hard put to think of one that is more in need than is the clergy of getting beyond the humdrum of unending pastoral duties, however rewarding they may sound on Blue-Monday reflections. The experience of ecstasy, though rarely common among mortals, and never, to my knowledge, among hospital chaplains, is said to be a perpetual delight of celestial beings as they frolic in the blissful presence of Deity.

On occasion, however, it is given to first this mortal and then that one to glimpse, for a fleeting moment, through the eye of personal experience, the blissful joy of ecstasy. And for that one solitary moment, the mystic and the poet are known to have labored for years. Sara Teasdale, hardly a mystic, though an unquestionably good poet, has described the value of ecstasy in these choice lines from her notable poem, "Barter":

> Spend all you have for loveliness,
>   Buy it and never count the cost;
> For one while singing hour of peace
>   Count many a year of strife well lost,
> And for a breath of ecstasy
>   Give all you have been, or could be.

Of course, the discriminating mind is justly quick in pointing out that ecstasy is both difficult, at best, to define and, when defined, is not frequently judged to be of any particularly practical value in the daily affairs of persons fully aware of their less than angelic nature. However, few clergy and fewer chaplains, in moments of rare but soul-cleansing candor, are unwilling to deny either their human frailties or their private pinings for the illusive encounter with ecstasy, and, failing ecstasy, at least a longing for a weekend away from the beloved yet bedeviling laity or the suspicious and bigoted physicians. Thus, the perpetual dilemma, whether to seek the practical and ever so mundane, boring, and benumbing syndrome fo the "day off" or the "clergy retreat," or the exuberatingly transcending experience and ever so cosmically catapulting journey into ecstasy.

Ecstasy is definable in a variety of equally meaningful ways, some more exotic and consequently less actualizable than others. Of those in the healing professions, few would claim ready experience of the exotic, even if all the while secretly wishing for at least "the unusual." But to go beyond mundane existence most would herald as a grand and welcomed accomplishment, particularly for those of us stultifying in our own provincialisms. Ecstasy offers the courageous adventurer into the inner chambers of the supramundane a purview on life that can truly be refreshing and liberating. Let us assume, therefore, that we are ready, in a practical exercise as opposed to fanciful musings, to define ecstasy as the capacity for, and experience of, "my distance from myself," a going beyond the mundane experience of self amidst society, or what I shall in this paper call *role distance*.

As relates to pastoral ecstasy, several flashes of valuable insight readily come to mind. The ministry is first and foremost a response to a Divine Call, and although I shall not open up this theological controversy, it does seem eumenically safe to say that all Christian bodies recognize the Divinely initiated nature of Holy Orders or ordination. Beyond (or might I say more correctly, "below") this Divine sanction of ordination, there is the actual historical person, the community, and the society within which ministry finds its common expression. Only at this level of time and space — the personal, the social, and the historical — can a sociologist claim to contribute to an understanding of ministry, ecstasy, and theapeutic duplicity.

ROLES, STATUSES, DEMEANORS, AND DEFERENCES

To speak of pastoral ecstasy is another way of suggesting role distance. A role is essentially a complex of commonly expected behavioral patterns that bespeak the positioning of an individual upon the social ladder. Needless to say, one's social status on this hierarchical continuum is maintained in accordance with one's roles, and, whether we like it or not, we are enmeshed in this social web of roles and statuses from the very first moment of our life.[1] During socially stable times, as for example, during the quiet 1950s, both role and status are easily determined and adhered to comfortably. That is to say, postmen, school teachers, clergy, housewives, etc., know reasonably well what is expected of them in their various arenas of daily activity and they usually comply, with at most a token of resistance. On the other hand, during times of acute social change, for example, during the late 1960s as graphically illustrated in such movie productions as "The Last Tango in Paris," "Easy Rider," and "The Godfather," the integrity and traditional authority of roles and statuses are severely challenged. In a real sense, virtually no one knows with certainty what is expected of him nor what to expect from others. To know where one stands in relation to others (i.e., status) and to be, therefore, able to understand what others rightfully can expect of oneself and what one can expect of others (i.e., role) is not only reassuring, but also a profoundly nurturing characteristic of a healthy society, the cost of health in this instance being the loss of the volatile excitement of erratic, erotic, exotic, and unpredictable bursts of social insanity in a frantic society in search of its lost soul.

During socially stable times, a role carries with it an expected demeanor, whereas a status carries a rightfully expected deference. Demeanor is that self-image portrayed to others through one's medley of roles, whereas deference is that response from others that one solicits with one's role-demeanor composite.[2] One's demeanor is illustrative of one's self-image — how one sees himself, defines his social position, etc. The socially universal law of oligarchy, called the Oligarchic Imperative, says that where two or more persons come together in a social relationship, a leader will emerge, taking to himself the role and status of leadership and, in response to his leadership demeanor, will elicit from his followers the deference worthy of his leadership and characteristic of followers.

Before we can attempt an understanding of pastoral ecstasy, therefore, we must first attempt to understand this sociological truism: namely, that no one is ever devoid of a multitude of roles, statuses, demeanors, and deferences. Furthermore, we are led to argue that discussions regarding "authentic" living are not well served by the pristinely naive suggestion that one must strip away one's roles in order to get at the "real" person as opposed to the "role" person, for, in spite of Rousseau and the candy-coated rhetoric of the touchy-feely psycho-clinicians of the "back to nature" tribe, the mature response to one's self-authenticity is a realization of, and an attempt to, respond critically to and direct the roles operative in one's own life. Clergy who deny the pervasive nature of this social truism in their own ministries are destined to perpetual frustration. It is patently impossible for the clergyman to "just be himself" when interacting with his congregants, for the simple reason that no individual can "just be himself" if by that notion we mean that a person can be stripped of all social roles and statuses. The sooner the clergy come to this realization, the sooner they will realize the importance of coming to personal grips with their vocation and its social ramifications for interaction.

All of this has important implications for the clergy, particularly for the realization of the importance of living creatively within and through this bundle of roles, statuses, demeanors, and deferences to which we are pathetically committed. That man is a social being and thus destined to carry the characteristics of his social nature is seen clearly in the experience of Robinson Crusoe who, even during his lonely existence on a desolate island, maintained sociocultural forms and expressions of value and meaning that would do any good Englishman proud. The native experience of the Noble Savage, devoid of socially entrapping contracts and customs, is only a fantasy of Rousseau and a figment in the anemic imagination of the counterculture struggling pathetically to realize the impossible on communal farms in Maine and musty caves in California. Truly, most of our life is spent bearing " one another's burdens," the burdens of ego, self-image, and social status. We should here call to mind the words of our Lord, who admonished us to "judge not" lest we be judged by the same judgment (Matt. 7:1ff). Man can know another, yea, himself also, only partially and too often ever so superficially, for only God in all His omniscience can know man definitively, even to the knowing of the unarticulated stirrings of our hearts and the ever-thinning growth of the scalp's turf.

Lest we too quickly forget, it is important to recall the importance of distinguishing between the pastoral call as an ontological category of theology, and the sociological consideration of the ministry as a social phenomenon. To attempt an analysis of the social dynamic characteristic of the ministry in the behavioral realm is significantly different from an analysis of the theological character of Holy Orders or ordination in the religious realm.

THE EXPERIENCE OF ROLE-DISTANCING

Ecstasy, I have proposed, is the experience of role-distancing, or the capacity of an individual to stand outside or above himself for purposes of critical reflection. The capacity for role-distancing is a potential quality for nurturing emotional well-being. The more emotionally healthy an individual is, the greater his ability in fruitfully exercising role-distance. To speak of role-distance is to imply that there is that of myself which stands above my roles, that of me which is forever judging, evaluating, selecting, and rejecting roles. If we define sin as "alienation from God," as David Roberts, along with a legion of others has done,[3] then we can anticipate that ecstasy serves the vital purpose of providing for us the experience of seeing ourselves as "others, even God" see us. For until we "come to ourselves" as did the Prodigal (Luke 15:11f.), we never move to that reflective level of self-awareness wherein shortcomings can be discerned. And whether or not we are able to "arise and go to [our] Father" as did the Prodigal, we can never address responsibly our failures and alienation or accept our maladies without this reflective self-awareness that results from role-distancing. If we cannot accept ourselves, Tillich has asked, how can we accept God's acceptance of us?[4] I am not suggesting here an "I'm-ok-you're-ok" syndrome of mutually reinforcing joy in sickness, but rather, a rigorously demanding cognizance of sin and the realization that man must, when confronted with sin's reality, face it responsibly or flee from it in fear. "The facing of short-comings, especially those which the individual cannot overcome," continues Roberts, "is never constructive except as he is allowed to uncover his problem in his own way." As with St. Peter and the denial scene before the crucifixion, until he gained some distance on the existential exigencies of the pressing moment of decision, he was operating at the pre-reflective level, the non-role-distance level. But, when he "remembered the words" of Jesus, says St. Matthew (Matt. 26:75), and "called to mind" what the Lord had said, says St. mark (Mark 14:72), he "thought thereon" and wept. Tears that follow reflection can cleanse the heart of sorrow and pain and prepare it to receive God's grace and blessing.

In opposition to materialistic behaviorism, which denies the existence of Transcendent Reality by contending that our "self" is conterminous with our "roles," I am arguing for something more profoundly humanistic, theistic, and, necessarily, Christocentric. Given the nature of the human condition wherein man (body, soul, spirit) finds himself localized in a particular time and place with a host of biological and sociological legacies, man is, from the beginning, faced with the struggle of making something good, productive, and meaningful out of his birthright. This biosocial legacy is the only means whereby our "authentic self," that self constituting the "real me" that transcends roles (the me I see as object), can find expression. It is through this body, immersed in its historically given biosocial milieu, that the person expresses himself. Though roles are the expressional medium of the self, there is no implicit justification for claiming, as do the behaviorists, that the self is simply coexistent with its repertoire of roles, no more than justly to argue that because my body is the physical agency of my expressional life that who I am is coextensive with my body. To a person with a body like Barney Phyfe this must sound like good news, but even the Raquel Welches and Elizabeth Taylors of this world are assuredly want to affirm that there is that of their true selves which cannot ultimately be expressed only by means of their physique. In opposition to Philip Rieff's praise of Freud's "doctrine of maturity...with its acceptance of meaninglessness as the end product of analytic wisdom,"[5] I concur with Outler that "in the Christian view of man, there could be no human selves apart from God — without a relation to God — because the ground and anchor point of the self's transcendence is in God (wherein is discovered) the spiritual origin and destiny of the self."[6] Or, in those immortal words of the Psalmist in Psalm 8, "What is man, that thou art mindful of him? And the son of man, that thou visitest him? For thou hast made him a little lower than the angels, and hast crowned him with glory and honour."

Furthermore, the healthier a person is emotionally, the greater the likelihood is of his awareness of this self-role relationship, and of there being in his personal life a genuinely creative interaction between his role-taking social self (the me I see as object) and his role-distancing authentic self (the I who sees the me as object). As Roberts has indicated, "The healing value of an insight is directly proportional to the degree in which the patient has made it his own instead of taking it over from another person."[7] As Israel could not successfully lean upon King Saul for protection in the same manner as their enemies leaned upon their kings, so neither can we become emotionally and spiritually healthy by continually leaning on others, never taking to ourselves the strength that has been given us in however meager proportions. There comes a time when we must pick up our five smooth stones and move into the battle. St. Paul has admonished us to bear one another's burdens and thereby fulfill the law of Christ, while St. James has told us to cast our cares upon Him, for he cares for us. The strength of pulling together is the strength of unified will and purpose, but in the experience of sharing, I must bring that which is me to the relationship if strength is to result. To claim another's strength as one's own, without offering one's own strength as belonging to the other, is thievery.

LEGITIMATE DUPLICITY

The capacity for, and experience of role-distance, i.e., the authentic self's supra-role suspension, is demonstrative of a natural self-role duplicity. Duplicity is, according to the *Oxford English Dictionary*, "the quality of being 'double' in action or conduct; the character or practice of acting in two ways at different times, or openly and secretly." Duplicity is essentially the ability to maintain two distinct identities simultaneously, and, within the context of the mundane-ecstatic continuum, duplicity is realized as the dual experience of, on the one hand, role-distancing via the authentic self and, on the other hand, role-taking via the social self. However, duplicity is of two kinds — legitimate and the more commonly thought of illegitimate. The latter, which Sartre likes to call "bad faith," is the conscious refusal on the part of the self to take responsibility for the realization of, and capacity for, role-distance. The discovery of the meaning and function of role-distance is, in a real sense, the discovery of personal freedom.

Both the Christian view of man and good sociology disallow a notion of complete human freedom, for man is bound in his action not only by the natural laws of physics and biology but also by social laws relating to social class, roles, statuses, etc. Furthermore, and more importantly, although man is responsible for his own ethical decisions and, therefore, in this respect free, he is not free to save himself from his condition, either from his biosocial legacy or from alienation from God. As Niebuhr has explained, man is free in that he knows of freedom and its absence in his own life.[8] Only man can know of freedom, and only man is free to know that he is not free and yet responsible. Man's fall resulted in his awareness of responsibility in freedom and the demise of freedom with irresponsibility.

"Those who hide freedom from themselves out of a 'spirit of seriousness' or by means of 'deterministic excuses,'" explains Sartre, "I shall call *cowards*; those who try to show that their existence is necessary, when it (their meager existence) is the very contingency of man's appearance on earth," he continues, "I shall call *stinkers*."[9] Two other cogent examples of illegitimate duplicity are the *zealot*, who refuses to stand outside his "cause," and the *charlatan*, who refuses to stand outside his "pretense" in the face of the experience of role-distance, thereby negating ethical responsibility in his treatment of others. "Man's reflection upon his predicament," explains Erich Fromm, "has led him to encounter two 'existential dichotomies,' or contradictions which man cannot annul but to which he must react"...viz., between life and death, and the realization that the span of human life is too short for the fulfillment of life.[10] Therefore, concludes Fromm, "Man is alone in a morally neutral universe. Man is, finally, his own and only moral referent."

Unfortunately, Fromm has taken a Sartrean leap in a Freudian parachute and has landed upon an untenable plot of sinking sand. With Rabbi Heschel, I hasten to argue, on the contrary, that if "you tell man that he is an end unto himself, his answer will be despair."[11] One need only recall the pitiful sight of a dejected and bewildered Freud in Nazi-occupied Vienna or an anxious and philosophically bankrupt Sartre in German-occupied Paris to realize that in the wake of faith in Transcendent Reality, despair moves in. We can only regret that Peter Homans' noble but unconvincing vindication of Freud has taken up this same Sartro-Freudian motif in his *Theology After Freud*.[12] Homans has taken up the task of giving account of what he has chosen to call the "collapse of the transcendent." "The self-authenticity and givenness of the spiritual reality of God" has, if Homans' analysis is correct, collapsed. We now see "the collapse of the doctrine of transcendence as a workable theological construct, the collapse of theology as a workable discipline and the collapse of the anguished conscience as the problematic ground for all theological self-understanding.... The modern self can no longer reflect upon itself and derive its sense of deepest validation from an appointed encounter with God the high." Or, if one wishes to speak crassly, Thank God we have buried God and freed ourselves from gratitude!

Freud and Sartre aside, however, we confront the possibility of a positively operative legitimate duplicity that is understood to be the ready willingness of an individual simultaneously to "stand outside" while being "responsible inside" his role, the stress of legitimate duplicity being "how to maintain integrity and keep on cheating." By cheating is meant the utilization of insight within a social encounter gained from an ecstatic perspective outside the social encounter. Legitimate duplicity, which is essentially our notion of personal ecstasy, necessarily requires the closest surveillance by the authentic self of its role choices. Roberts again says: "Therapy has a moral purpose because it rests on the assumption that internal harmony and a capacity for personal growth and responsibility are better than emotional conflict, anxiety, and self-enslavement. In serving this purpose, [therapy] is fostering a humanitarian end which is analogous to religious salvation."[13] Through this ongoing process of self-role verification, emotional health is continually being nurtured. Through ecstacy realized by means of legitimate duplicity, the human possibilities of life are perceived more clearly. "The human possibility," says Outler,

> is the growth in spontaneity and vitality of man's freedom, his intelligence, and his love. It is the life of faith, in which men rely on, and relax in the dynamic action of God's creation and redemption. It is the life of hope, the confidence that God has the power to achieve His will and has a will of love and concern for man, even in his rebellion and self-defeat. It is the life of love, human love which has been called out and ennobled by God's love, who first loved us and launched this strange human enterprise on its precarious journey.[14]

Authentic living is the realization of personal ecstasy through legitimate duplicity. If illegitimate duplicity is "bad faith," then legitimate duplicity is "honest commitment." But honest commitment as realized in legitimate duplicity, is in a paradoxical sense "cheating," by which one utilizes a perspective toward social relations beyond which and above which others have not attained. The thrill of cheating is the pastoral joy of ecstatic living. The honesty of the self standing *above* its roles is called *supra-role authenticity*, whereas the honesty of the self *choosing roles* consistent with its value commitments is called *pan-role authenticity*. Authentic living is ecstatic living — a life-enduring experience of role taking and role-distancing. To stand outside and above one's many roles not only offers an opportunity for critical evaluation but also, and more importantly, provides an indispensable medium for authentic living by aligning one's roles in accordance with one's true self. Knowing oneself not only means plumbing the depths of the authentic self (the I who sees me as object) but also means monitoring the social self (the me that I see as object) in accordance with my self validating authenticity. The authentic self is an *ontological possibility*, the social self is an *operational inevitability*, and the awareness of both selves and the creative coordination of both is the gift of ecstasy.

Sara Teasdale concludes her poem with this admonition:

> And for a breath of ecstasy,
> Give all you have been, or could be.

NOTES

1.   Cf. George J. McCall and J. L. Simmons, *Identities and Interactions* (New York: Collier-Macmillan, 1966), pp. 125-66; and Robert K. Merton, *Social Theory and Social Structure* (New York: Free Press, 1968), pp. 122-34.

2.   Erving Goffman, "The Nature of Deference and Demeanor," *American Anthropologist* 58 (1956):47-85. Cf. S. Frank Miyamoto and Sandford M. Dorn-Busch, "A Test of Interactionist Hypotheses of Self-Conception," *American Journal of Sociology* 61 (1965): 399-403.

3.   David E. Roberts, *Psychotherapy and A Christian View of Man* (New York: Charles Scribners, 1950), p. 110.

4.   Paul Tillich, *The Courage To Be* (New Haven: Yale Paperbacks, 1967), p. 166.

5. Philip Rieff, *The Triumph of the Therapeutic* (New York: Harper Torchbooks, 1968), p. 43.

6. Albert C. Outler, *Psychotherapy and the Christian Message* (New York: Harper Chapelbook, 1966), pp. 69, 59.

7. Roberts, *Psychotherapy*, p. 4.

8. Reinhold Niebuhr, *The Nature and Destiny of Man* (New York: Charles Scribners, 1964), vol. 1, *Human Nature*, pp. 250-64.

9. Jean-Paul Sartre, *Existentialism and Human Emotions* (New York: Philosophical Library, 1957), p. 46.

10. Erich Fromm, *Man for Himself* (New York: Fawcett, 1973), pp. 38-58.

11. Abraham J. Heschel, *Who Is Man?* (Stanford: University Press, 1963), p. 78.

12. Peter Homans, *Theology After Freud* (New York: Bobbs-Merrill, 1970), p. 168.

13. Roberts, *Psychotherapy*, p. 40.

14. Outler, *Psychotherapy*, p. 180.

APPENDIX C

MEANING AS HERMENEUTICS:
The Interpretation Imperative

Everywhere in the modern world is evidenced an almost frantic compulsion for mankind to understand himself and his world. Whether we peruse the latest works in literature, art, or music, the result is the same — man seeks to understand himself and his world. But such understanding, though sought after with passionate drive, continually eludes him. "The tragedy of modern man," says Abraham J. Heschel in venturing to explain modern man's present crisis, "is that he thinks alone."[1] In mankind's frantic search to understand himself and his relationship to his world, he is continually baffled and mystified by his persisting inability to define himself in terms relevant to his humanity, terms larger than himself with power to draw him forward into the future. "The greatest challenge of modern man," explains Teilhard de Chardin, "is to establish an abiding faith in the future."[2]

But in order for such a faith to emerge, man must not only have a singularly personal sense of "What am I?," but also a universally social sense of "Who is Man?" "No age," observes Martin Heidegger, "has known so much, and so many different things, about man as ours...And no age has known less than ours of what man is."[3] The problem, as Heidegger so clearly sees, is not a deficiency in technical knowledge, in scientific information, in bio-medical and psycho-social aptitude and insight, but rather the problem is deeper and lies behind all this burgeoning of knowledge, information, aptitudes and insights. The problem is not man's intellect. The problem is man himself. Knowledge of the world seems not to be a problem, but the understanding of man himself and his relationship to the world does. "We are the first epoch," observes Scheler, "in which man has become fully and thoroughly 'problematic' to himself; in which he no longer knows what he essentially is, but at the same time also knows that he does not know."[4]

Of course, to know that one does not know is one step towards addressing the problem responsibly. What seems to be absent from the modern experience is any context or frame of reference within which, or from which, judgements can be made with conviction, a position from which lives can be lived with authenticity. "The most poignant problem of modern life," explains the Nobel Prize winning biologist, René Dubos, "is probably man's feeling that life has lost significance."[5] The gradual encroachment of pervasive relativism — a sense that nothing is any more or less significant than anything else — seems to have successfully assaulted man's own self-image more so than any of his particular ideologies or industries.

And when man looks to his ancient past for some root from which to regain strength to carry on and renew his vigor to reaffirm the humanness of his being, mankind falters. What was perceived in days of resoluteness to be way-markers in man's self-understanding degenerates in days of self-doubt to little more than halfhearted speculations. When men are strong, they revere their past for the power they see there; but when men falter, their past too loses power. As the French philosopher Ernst Cassirer has so painfully pointed out, "Nowhere in Plato's Socratic dialogues do we find a direct solution to the problem, 'What is man?' There is only an indirect answer, 'Man is declared to be that creature who is constantly in search of himself — a creature who in every moment of his existence must examine and scrutinize the conditions of his existence."[6]

From Plato we learn little about the nature of man, but we learn much about that which makes man human. His humanity is manifest in his drive to know, as Aristotle once said centuries ago — to know who he is and what his relationship is to the world. "He is a being in search of meaning," says Heschel.[7] And, in seeking to know himself, man defines his world. He interprets his world in terms of his own humanity. Throughout history, the human crisis has always centered around man's search for himself, for meaning, a meaning which derives from his propensity to interpret. By virtue of interpreting his world, man creates a history, and history for man is the record of his discovery of meaning for himself within his world. And meaning in turn becomes the mechanism whereby he continues to understand and interpret. A discussion of this development, of man interpreting himself and his world in terms of relationship-as-meaning, is the purpose of this chapter.

In man's quest to understand himself, in his drive to examine and scrutinize the conditions of his existence, to come to grips with his world, he must inevitably engage in interpretation. Man confronts a world of reality which, if he is to survive and thrive, he must interpret. The issue is not so much whether he creates or discovers order and purpose in this world of reality, as the fact that this reality (real or imagined) compels him to encounter it and interpret it. "I believe," says Marias, "that the universe is covered by a patina of interpretations."[8] Of course, what is not being implied here is that reality is merely interpretation. On the contrary, "reality is something that makes me make interpretation (emphasis mine)." The human quality of the lived experience in the world of reality is fundamentally interpretational. Man never achieves a sense of this reality without interpretation.

Amidst this frantic compulsion to know himself by means of interpreting the world, we must not suppose that mankind's humanity has any analogue in the physical environment from which to draw comparisons. Whereas the physical — the sub-human environment — can be described in terms of its objective properties, Cassirer argues cogently that "man may be described and defined only in terms of his consciousness."[9] That which so decisively differentiates the physical world of reality from the human world of reality is consciousness — man's reflective self awareness. Teilhard de Chardin once observed that the difference between man and animal is that the latter "knows," but the former "knows that he knows."[10]

Though man, as animal, encounters his world as a physical reality, man, as human, encounters his world as an interpreted reality. This distinctiveness of man vis-à-vis animal is not merely a quantitative leap in breadth of worlds perceived, but is a qualitative leap in depth of worlds experienced. Whereas man, like other animals, employs receptor and effector systems of bio-physical adaptation to his physical environment, man alone has discovered the symbolic system as explained so cogently by Cassirer. "This new acquisition transforms the whole of human life...As compared with other animals man lives not merely in a broad reality; he lives, so to speak, in a new dimension of reality."[11] We might wish to call this a *mileiu symbolicum*.

This new dimension of reality is a discovery of man resulting from his drive to interpret his world — an encounter with the symbolic dimension of a world perceived in abstract space. This is the distinctive character of the human species, that it has developed the capacity for abstraction through symbolization, and in abstracting from the physical world, man interprets the symbolic world known only to himself. And herein lies the humanness of man's encounter with, and desire to understand this new dimension, this symbolic world, which demands not only a subject-object encounter, but an interpretation. "Wherever a man dreams or raves," explains Paul Ricouer, "another man arises to give an interpretation; what was already discourse, even if incoherent, is brought into coherent discourse by hermeneutics."[12] Man manifests his humanity by interpreting, not just reacting, to his environment, i.e., human experience seeking understanding.

As noted earlier, the modern crisis is one of meaning, man's inability to interpret his world in a manner that makes what he does, thinks, and dreams make a difference. "The concept of meaning," suggests Langer, "in all its varieties, is the dominant philosophical concept of our time."[13] The dominance of the concept of meaning bespeaks the pervasiveness of the perceived problem. Man is in search of his own humanity, or in the words of Carl Gustav Jung, "Modern man in search of a soul."[14]

And in the search, and within the new dimension of symbol, mankind requires a sense of orderliness, predictability, rationality, understandability. "Men are congenitally compelled," says Berger, "to impose a meaningful order upon reality."[15] Though I had rather say man is compelled to discover a meaningful order within reality, nevertheless, the "propensity for order...(is) one fundamental human trait" which is crucial in understanding the compulsions of man to interpret as meaningful the world of reality.[16]

It should be evident by now that what I mean by understanding through interpretation is not simply an explanation of the world as man encounters it. Long ago, Dilthey cleared up the matter of distinguishing between explanation and understanding as applied to human awareness. "We explain," says he, "by means of purely intellectual processes, but we understand by means of the combined activities of all the mental powers in apprehending...We explain nature; **man we must understand** (emphasis mine)."[17] We can say then that in the act of understanding man's nature, he comes through mental effort to comprehend living human experience.

Only man can have a crisis of meaning, for only man can understand his world by interpreting the complexities of his encounter with the new dimension of the milieu symbolicum. And in this dimension, which he interprets, man confronts the historical nature of his being in the world. Richard Palmer has aided us along this train of thought by focusing not only upon Cassirer's description of man as animal symbolicum but also, and concomitantly upon, man's compulsion to interpret this new dimension of reality. "In hermeneutical theory," Palmer explains, "man is seen as dependent on constant interpretation of the past, and thus it could almost be said that man is the 'hermeneutical animal,' who understands himself in terms of interpreting a heritage and shared world bequeathed him from the past, a heritage constantly present and active in all his actions and decision."[18] It is in historical consciousness that man becomes fully human and necessarily confronts his own humanness. By virtue of his compulsion to interpret a world he desires to understand, a world limited to his capacity for abstraction through symbolization, man discovers history. "In historicality," says Palmer, "modern hermeneutics finds its theorectical foundations."

In man's desire to know, to come not merely to an explanation of his physical environment, but to understand by interpretation the symbolic dimension of reality which he alone has discovered, he is inevitably confronted with the emergence of an historical consciousness. "Man has no nature," Ortega y Gassett once said, "what he has is history."[19] Certainly what has been presented here thus far is not so much an attempt to definitionally circumscribe human nature, so much as to characterize the human propensity as interpretation, as hermeneutical, as symbolic, as historical. Heidegger said in deference to Dilthey's enamoration of history that   "historical understanding is something belonging to the way of being man." We have seen that with the emergence of consciousness, i.e., reflective self-awareness, within the human species a new dimension of reality has been discovered, understood, and interpreted such that an historical sensibility is an inevitable and indispensable corollary of man's own humanity.

With the overall effort here being to illustrate that man's propensity to interpret his world rests upon a sense of history as meaning and meaning as hermeneutic, Palmer has said that the "hermeneutical experience is intrinsically historical."[20] As noted earlier, man, unlike animals, confronts an objective world which he encounters not only with his receptor and effector sensory systems, but unlike other animals, man also, and distinguishingly, encounters an abstract world of symbols.   "Ideal reconstruction," says Cassirer, "not empirical observation, is the first step in historical knowledge...(For) the historian finds at the very beginning of his research a symbolic universe."[21] It is at the level of historical knowledge that man so uniquely distinguishes himself above the physical world of animal life. Man interprets what he encounters, and his interpretation is historical in character.

The interpretation of man's place in the world is essentially an expression of his perception of relationships — relationships as embodying a sense of life's meaning. "The component parts of what comprises our view of the progression of our life (*Auschauung es Lebensverlaufes*)," explains Dilthey, "are all contained together in living itself."[22] Whereas Kantians would have us believe that this inner temporality or historicality is superimposed from a priori mental categories, we would rather argue for their being intrinsic to man's world as Dilthey and Heidegger, among others, have so convincingly argued in modern times. The point is crucial to all hermeneutics and is determinative for our work. "Experience," explains Palmer, "is intrinsically temporal (historical), and therefore understanding of experience must also be in commensurately temporal categories of thought."[23]

Historicality (*Geschichtlichkeit*) as used here, is formed by Dilthey's thesis that "what man is only history can tell him."[24] The term usually carries a dual meaning, discussed at length by Otto Friedrich Bollnow, viz., first, the fact that man understands himself not so much through introspection as through the objectification of life, and second, that man's nature is not a fixed essence, but rather that in the phrase of Dilthey, man is a "not-yet-determined animal" (*noch nicht festgestellte tier*).[25] Thus we see the inevitability of man's interpretation of his world, being an expression of his quest for meaning, as an historical event. The intrinsic temporality of understanding itself, as Heidegger has argued, is in seeing the world always in terms of past, present, and future. This we are calling the historicality of understanding. "Meaning," Palmer has suggested, "always stands in a horizontal context...(such that) the concept of 'historicality'...comes to refer not only to man's dependence on history for his self-understanding and self-interpretation but also to the inseparability of history and the intrinsic temporality of all understanding."[26]

Understanding, Heidegger has taught us, is the basis for all interpretation. By understanding, he would have us mean man's power to grasp his own "possibilities for being" within the "lifeworld of our existence." As Heidegger sees it, understanding operates within a set of already interpreted relationships, or in Heidegger's own term, "relational whole (*Bewandtnisganzheit*)." And, whereas understanding implies interpreted relationships, Dilthey has earlier suggested that meaningfulness is always a matter of reference to a "context of relationships (*Strukturzusammenhaug*)."

Historicality as man's interpretation of his perceived relationships to the world and himself manifests itself in terms of man's quest for meaning. Human history, we are suggesting, is the result of man's interpretation of perceived relationships — his grasp through interpretation of meaning. "History," Cassirer once said, "is relationship (meaning) understood." Meaning is the essence of history as history is the essence of human interpretation of the new dimension of reality, a dimension which can only be understood and interpreted in terms of the experiential category of meaning. "Meaning," continues Palmer, "is the name given to different kinds of relationships."[27]

It is at this juncture, of history as meaning, that man's nature so poignantly manifests and reveals itself. In grasping his world — relation as meaning — man grasps himself, the maker of history and the discoverer of its meaning. "History is not knowledge of external facts or events," explains Cassirer, "it is a form of self-knowledge...In history man constantly returns to himself."[28] As man is compelled to interpret his newly discovered milieu symbolicum, he comes to know that the meaning of history is most exactly the history of meaning, a process whereby man, interpreting his abstract environment, comes to a working definition of himself. "Not through introspection," says Dilthey, "but only through history do we come to know ourselves."[29]

It is through interpretation, says Heidegger, that man confronts the problem and meaning of his own being. "The logos of a phenomenology of Dasein," explains Heidegger, "has the character of *hermeneuein* (to interpret), through which are made known to Dasein the structure of his own being and the authentic meaning of being given in his (preconscious) understanding of being."[30] Therefore, we might convincingly argue that historicality — man's consciousness of the sequential nature of interpretation — constitutes the proper milieu for man's self-understanding. And, therefore, in interpretation, i.e., hermeneutics, we find man's best efforts at finding, within the context of the quest for meaning, the nature of his own being. "Phenomenology of Dasein," continues Heidegger, "is hermeneutics in the original sense of the words, which designates the business of interpretation...Hermeneutics," concludes Heidegger, "has become interpretation of the being of Dasein."

If Heidegger has strengthened our belief that hermeneutics as interpretation of the being of Dasein is indispensable in man's quest for self-knowledge, then Dilthey has vindicated our sense of history as meaning, the experiential framework of relationships embodying the meaningfulness of existence interpreted and understood. In experience itself, temporality is expressed in the context of relationship, for experience is not a static phenomenon, but rather, "in its unity of meaning it (experience) tends to reach out and encompass both recollection of the past and anticipation of the future in the total context of 'meaning.'"[31]

Historical consciousness emerged within the context of a human experience of compulsion to interpret the abstracted relationships and realities of a symbolic world. And in the emergence of this consciousness, man came to realize that the meaning of this compulsion, the meaning of this history, was really the history of man's meaning. "Meaning," Dilthey pointed out, "cannot be imagined...(rather) the past and the future form a structural unity with the presentness of all experience, and perception in the present is interpreted."[32] In this discovery of meaning, revealed in history to man through his drive to know his world by interpreting it, man has discovered the means by which life can be grasped. The meaning of the being of Dasein is within human reach.

The crisis of modern man, we have been saying, is a crisis of meaning. Man, due to techno-scientific and psycho-cosmic factors which will not be analyzed here, has lost the capacity, not to explain, but to understand his world and to interpret his relationship to it meaningfully. A failure of historical conscious-ness has bludgeoned man into a state of existential unconsciousness. The task for modern man, if he would regain a sense of resolute purposefulness and unequivocal directionability to his life, is to recover a consciousness of historicality (*Geschichtlichkeit*) of his own existence. Dilthey has convinc-ingly suggested that life is experience in "individual moments of meaning," and that these moments of meaning "require the context of the past and the horizon of future expectations..." which can only be explained and understood in terms of the human dimension of historicality.[33] An understanding of the character and quality, origin and direction, of these "moments of meaning" is what our discussion of man as interpreter, interpretation as history, and history as meaning is all about. To illustrate how the concept of meaning can be employed as a *hermeneutical device* in grasping the meaning of our being is our last and pivotal point in this discussion, viz., meaning as hermeneutics.

The humanness of man is exemplified in his drive and ability to encounter and interpret a new dimension of reality beyond the physical environment, a world of symbols embodying an intrinsically historical discovery of meaning. Not only does human life illustrate the meaning of history, human life also embodies the history of meaning. "The dimension of meaning," explains Heschel, "is as indigenous to man's being human as the dimension of space is to stars and stones."³⁴ If our scenario is correct this far — man as interpreter, interpretation as history, history as meaning — then we are led resolutely to the crowning postulate of this development which is that meaning for man, whether created or discovered, is the interpretive mechanism par excellence by which he lives. *Meaning is hermeneutics.*

Technically speaking, "hermeneutics is the study of understanding," or more precisely, hermeneutics "is the study of the methodological principles of interpretation and explanation." Yet, though these definitions are correct in the academic sense of the word, they fail to reach at the heart of my intention. They fall short of the existentially human quality of my aphorism — meaning as hermeneutics. Closer to the point is Ricouer's suggestion that "hermeneutics is the system by which the deeper significance is revealed beneath the manifest content."³⁶

Our intention in developing this thought has led us to Heidegger's notion of the "hermeneutics of Dasein" outlined in the *Sein Und Zeit* (1927). Here, we see the temporality and existential roots of understanding which form the backdrop for man's interpretation of the meaningfulness of his being. Hermeneutics for Heidegger is the study of the understanding of the works of man, or more pointedly, an explanation of human existence itself. Interpretation as well as understanding are foundational modes of man's being. And the followers of Heidegger see hermeneutics as a philosophical exploration of the character and requisite conditions for all understanding and interpretation.³⁷

Heidegger's contribution to hermeneutics is unquestionably significant, having marked a turning point in the development of both the term and the field. Hermeneutics has become at once linked both to the ontological and the existential dimensions of understanding and interpretation. Now, the definition of hermeneutics, thanks to Heidegger, deals with "the moment that meaning comes to light." In these moments, man interprets his world in terms of meaning, i.e., meaning as hermeneutics. And, these moments, as expressive of the historicality of man, are both cultural and religious in the sense that culture and religion are meaning-systems by means of which man grasps the new dimension of his own being in the world.

Meaning, as discussed earlier, carries with it the element of historicality, of temporality. Meaning does not exist merely in the abstract but profoundly manifests itself in the concrete, in the lived experience of the human community. Necessarily, then, if meaning is to function hermeneutically as the human mechanism for interpreting the world, meaning must function through those arenas of human experience most directly linked to encountering a world in need of interpretation. Those arenas are culture and religion.

The Princeton anthropologist, Clifford Geertz, has defined "man as a symbolizing, conceptualizing, meaning-seeking animal,"[38] who produces culture and religion as expressions of these characteristics. Culture, explains Geertz, is "an historically transmitted pattern of meanings embodied in symbols."[39] Accordingly, religion "is in part an attempt to conserve the fund of general meanings in terms of which each individual interprets his experience and organizes his conduct." In the same context, Geertz has suggested that man's compulsion to "make sense out of experience" is as characteristically human as man's biological needs. Thus, "to make sense out of experience" is what, in the Heideggerian sense, we are labeling hermeneutics, and it is by means of the meaning-systems of culture and religion that this "drive to interpret" most predictably, systematically, and fruitfully reveals itself.

We have been suggesting that meaning is the hermeneutical device or key by which man interprets his world, in the sense that hermeneutics in the Heideggerian usage, is "the analysis of human existence."[40] Whereas among the anthropologists, Geertz would propose that culture-analysis must focus upon the meaning-system embodied in cultural symbols, philosophers and theologians might likewise argue that religious-analysis must focus upon the meaning-system embodied in religious symbols. Heinrich Otto, a modern theologian, reportedly has said that "theology is really hermeneutics," whereas

Carl Michaelson, another modern theologian, has suggested that systematic theology is "the hermeneutical analysis of being."

If Geertz is the modern anthropological exemplar of culture-analysis employing the concept of meaning as the interpretive key in his science, then Paul Tillich is unquestionably the modern theological exemplar of religious analysis employing the concept of meaning as the interpretive key in his discipline.[41] For Tillich, meaning is that from which all religious and cultural expressions receive their impetus. And he was, therefore, very impatient with any notion of a meaningless existence — for him a notion impossible to entertain or defend. "Even the totality of meaning," Tillich once argued, "need not be meaningful, but rather could disappear, like every particular meaning in the abyss of meaninglessness, if the presupposition of an unconditional meaningfulness were not alive in every act of meaning."[42] For Tillich, to raise the question or possibility of meaninglessness is to have already posited meaning.

Contrary to Sartre's existentialism,[43] Tillich insists that meaning is not a creation of man's own devices but rather a discovery which reveals the sustaining source of the human spirit. "Culture," reasons Tillich, "does not create this empty space of mere validity. It creates meaning as the actualization of what is potential in the bearer of the spirit — in man."[44] Culture is not self-contained, but rather points beyond its symbol-systems to that from which it derives its power for human creativity. Tillich argues that both culture and religion are meaning-systems, are mechanisms expressed through symbols by the human spirit, which converge in the creativity of man's quest to interpret his world. "Religion," he explains, "is directedness toward the Unconditional (the Unconditional meaning, toward the import of meaning), and culture is directedness toward the conditioned forms (of meaning) and their unity."[45] Having framed the relationship of culture and religion in terms of their shared convergence upon meaning as man's effort to grasp his world, Tillich has added another dimension to Geertz's approach to culture and religion analysis. Thus, Tillich establishes a symbiotic relationship between religion and culture in these terms: "In the cultural act, the religious is substantial; in the religious act, the cultural is formal."[46]

If culture is the experiential expression of meaning, or more correctly, is the context within which, and the socio-historical mechanism whereby, meaning is both experienced and expressed, then the function of the concept of meaning is necessarily interpretational, or hermeneutical.[47] In closing, we might suggest that religion as an expression of meaning is a demonstration of mankind's quest to know and understand his world and his place in it. We might then, on the basis of the foregoing discussion, propose a set of definitions. Culture is that integrated complex of conceptual and empirical expressions of conditional and created meaning embodied within a socio-historical milieu. Religion is that integrated complex of conceptual and empirical expressions of unconditional and discovered meaning embodied within a socio-historical milieu.[48] By having defined religion and culture as meaning-systems, as arenas within which expressions of meaning converge, we have demonstrated the religio-cultural matrix of interpretation — an interpretation of man's historicality wherein we can define religion and culture as meaning, and meaning as hermeneutics.[49]

NOTES

1.   Abraham Joshua Heschel, *Who is Man?* (Stanford, CA: Stanford University Press, 1968), p. 76.

2.   Teilhard de Chardin, *Building the Earth* (NY: Avon Books, 1965), p. 105.

3.   Martin Heidegger, *Kant Und Das Problem Der Metaphysik* (Frankfort: Klostermann, 1951).

4.   As quoted in Martin Buber, *Between Man and Man* (NY: Macmillan: 1968), p. 182.

5.   Rene Dubos, *So Human an Animal* (NY: Charles Scribner's Sons, 1968), p. 14.

6.   Ernst Cassirer, *An Essay on Man* (New Haven: Yale University Press, 1969), p. 5.

7.   Abraham Joshua Heschel, *The Insecurity of Freedom: Essays on Human Existence* (NY: Schocken Books, 1972), p. 162.

8. Julian Marias, "Philosophic Truth and the Metaphoric System," in *Interpretation: The Poetry of Meaning*, edited by Stanley Romaine Hopper and D. L. Miller (NY: Harcourt, Brace & World, 1967), p. 48.

9. Cassirer, *Essay on Man*, p. 5.

10. For discussion see my "Ethnicity and the Future of Man: The Perspective of Teilhard de Chardin," *The Teilhard Review XI*, 1 (Feb, 19976): 16-21.

11. Cassirer, *Essay on Man*, p. 24.

12. Paul Ricouer, "The Symbol Gives Rise to Thought," in *Literature and Religion*, edited by G. B. Gunn (NY: Harper Forum, 1971), p. 213.

13. Susanne K. Langer, *Philosophical Sketches* (NY: Mentor Books, 1964), p. 54.

14. Carl Gustav Jung, *Modern Man in Search of a Soul* (NY: Harcourt, Brace, and World, 1933).

15. Peter L. Berger, the *Sacred Canopy: Elements of a Socio-Logical Theory of Religion* (NY: Anchor, 1969), p. 22.

16. Peter L. Berger, *A Rumor of Angels: Modern Society and the Rediscovery of the Sacred* (NY: Anchor, 1970), p. 53.

17. Wilhelm Dilthey, *Gesammelte Schriften*, 14 volumes (Gottingen: Vandenhoeck and Ruprecht, 1913-1967), V:172.

18. Richard E. Palmer, *Hermeneutics: Interpretation Theory in Schleiermacher, Dilthey, Heidegger, and Gadamer* (Evanston, IL: Northwestern University Press, 1969), p. 118. Also see my "Religious Myth and Symbol: A Convergence of Philosophy and Anthropology," *Philosophy Today*, XVIII, 4 (Spring, 1974): 68-84.

19. As quoted in Cassirer, *Essay on Man*, p. 172.

150   John H. Morgan

20. Palmer, *Hermeneutics*, p. 242.

21. Cassirer, *Essay on Man*, pp. 174-175.

22. Dilthey, *Gesammelte Schriften*, VII:224.

23. Palmer, *Hermeneutics*, p. 111.

24. Dilthey, *Gesammelte Schriften*, VIII:224.

25. Otto Friedrich Bollnow, *Die Lebensphilosophie* (Berlin: Springer, 1958).

26. Palmer, *Hermeneutics*, p. 117.

27. Ibid., p. 120.

28. Cassirer, *Essay on Man*, p. 191.

29. Dilthey, *Gesammelte Schriften*, VII:279.

30. Martin Heidegger, *Sein Und Ziet* (Halle: Niemeyer, 1927), p. 37.

31. Dilthey as quoted by Palmer, *Hermeneutics*, p. 109.

32. Dilthey, *Gesammelte Schriften*, VI:317.

33. Dilthey as quoted by Palmer, *Hermeneutics*, p. 101.

34. Heschel, *Who is Man?*, p. 51.

35. *Webster's Third New International Dictionary.*

36. Palmer, *Hermeneutics*, p. 44.

37. Heidegger's hermeneutics is carefully analyzed by Hans-Georg Gadamer, *Wahrheit Und Methode: Grunzuge Einer Philodophischen Hermeneutik* (Tubingen: J.C.B. Mohr, 1960).

38. Clifford Geertz, "Ethos, World-View and the Analysis of the Sacred Symbols," *Antioch Review* (Winter, 1957-58): 436.

39. Clifford Geertz, "Religion as a Cultural System," in *Anthropological Approaches to the Study of Religion*, edited by M. Banton (Longon: Tavistock, 1966, p. 3.

40. Stanley Romaine Hopper, "The Poetry of Meaning," in *Literature and Religion*, p. 223.

41. For a critical comparison of Tillich and Geertz on this point, see Chapter Ten above, pp. 136 ff.

42. Paul Tillich, *What is Religion?* (NY: Harper, 1969), p. 57.

43. For a critique of Sartre's use of the concept of "meaning," see my *In Search of Meaning: From Freud to Teilhard De Chardin* (Washington, D.C.: University Press of America, 1978), pp. 15-23.

44. Paul Tillich, *Systematic Theology*, 3 volumes (Chicago: University of Chicago Press, 1967), III:84.

45. Tillich, *What is Religion?*, p. 59.

46. Ibid., p. 60.

47. See my "Clifford Geertz: An Interfacing of Anthropology and Religious Studies," *Horizons*, V, 2 (Winter, 1978): 203-210.

48. This point is considered carefully in my "Theology and Symbol: An Anthropological Approach," *Journal of Religious Thought*, XXX, 3 (Fall, 1974): 51-61.

49.   Cf. My latest book on this topic, *Interfacing Geertz and Tillich* (Orissa: Mayur Publichers, 1997).

QUESTIONNAIRE AND DATA CHARTS

A. THE R.I.O. STUDY

The Rome-Indiana-Oxford Clergy Time Conflict Study

REMARKS ... Thanks to a research grant from the Zycon Corporation of America, a major data-base study of time conflicts in today's ministry is being conducted in the United States. Growing out of deliberations with clergy held in Rome, Oxford, and Indiana, the following questionnaire has been developed as the first stage in this national survey. We need your help as your name has been drawn from a national data-base of clergy in one of three control traditions –Anglican, Catholic, Lutheran, or Methodist. If you would take ten minutes to complete this questionnaire and return in the self-addressed stamped envelop, you would be rendering THE R.I.O. STUDY a great service. Your anonymity is assured. Availability of the published study will be announced in the national press sometime late next summer. Thank you, again, for your kind assistance in this major research project.

INSTRUCTIONS ... For each of the following activities, you are asked to mark THREE separate answers, one on each of three separate charts. You are to mark (1) the TIME ALLOCATION CHART (TAC) indicating how many hours (rounded off to the next hour with any part of an hour considered a full hour) you spend in each identified activity; you are to mark the VALUE ASSESSMENT CHART (VAC) for (2) your best guess as to your parish's value placed on each designated activity, indicating on a range of one to five (1-5) the least desired to the most desired, and (3) your own individual value placed on each of the same activities, indicating the least to the most desired ranking. PLACE AN "X" OVER THE BLOCK INDICATING YOUR BEST ANSWER ON ALL THREE CHARTS.

(EXAMPLE) Mowing your lawn.

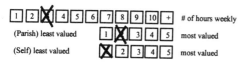

| 1 | 2 | ☒ | 4 | 5 | 6 | 7 | 8 | 9 | 10 | + | # of hours weekly |

(Parish) least valued | 1 | ☒ | 3 | 4 | 5 | most valued

(Self) least valued   ☒ | 2 | 3 | 4 | 5 | most valued

QUESTIONNAIRE

(Fill in the blanks on the following five items of basic biographical information.)

1. Age _____   Gender _____   Ethnicity _____

2. Years in the ordained ministry _____

3. Post-ordination academic/professional degrees (initials only) _____

4. Your religious tradition: Anglican _____   Catholic _____
                               Methodist _____   Lutheran _____

5. In order of importance to your own personal ministry, rank the following three descriptions of ministry self-images using (1) for most important and (3) for least important. Scholar _____   Priest _____   Pastor _____

(In the following list of activities, please be sure to mark all three charts of activities.)

1. Preparing the Sunday homily or sermon.
    [1] [2] [3] [4] [5] [6] [7] [8] [9] [10] [+]   # of hours weekly
    (Parish) least valued   [1] [2] [3] [4] [5]   most valued
    (Self) least valued   [1] [2] [3] [4] [5]   most valued

2. Studying/reading major theologians of the day.
    [1] [2] [3] [4] [5] [6] [7] [8] [9] [10] [+]   # of hours weekly
    (Parish) least valued   [1] [2] [3] [4] [5]   most valued
    (Self) least valued   [1] [2] [3] [4] [5]   most valued

3. Systematic, regular exegetical study of Scripture.
    [1] [2] [3] [4] [5] [6] [7] [8] [9] [10] [+]   # of hours weekly
    (Parish) least valued   [1] [2] [3] [4] [5]   most valued
    (Self) least valued   [1] [2] [3] [4] [5]   most valued

4. Serving as a spokesperson of authority for the teachings of the Church.
    [1] [2] [3] [4] [5] [6] [7] [8] [9] [10] [+]   # of hours weekly
    (Parish) least valued   [1] [2] [3] [4] [5]   most valued
    (Self) least valued   [1] [2] [3] [4] [5]   most valued

5. Functioning as a valued and respected intellectual within the life of the parish.
    [1] [2] [3] [4] [5] [6] [7] [8] [9] [10] [+]   # of hours weekly
    (Parish) least valued   [1] [2] [3] [4] [5]   most valued
    (Self) least valued   [1] [2] [3] [4] [5]   most valued

1. Leading the congregation in public worship.
    [1] [2] [3] [4] [5] [6] [7] [8] [9] [10] [+]   # of hours weekly
    (Parish) least valued   [1] [2] [3] [4] [5]   most valued
    (Self) least valued   [1] [2] [3] [4] [5]   most valued

2. Presiding over the Eucharist/Holy Communion/Lord's Supper.
    [1] [2] [3] [4] [5] [6] [7] [8] [9] [10] [+]   # of hours weekly
    (Parish) least valued   [1] [2] [3] [4] [5]   most valued
    (Self) least valued   [1] [2] [3] [4] [5]   most valued

3. Exercising "Sacramental" functions of ministry such as hearing confessions, baptising, absolutions, anointing the sick, etc. (excluding from this time frame Eucharistic celebrations).

| 1 | 2 | 3 | 4 | 5 | 6 | 7 | 8 | 9 | 10 | + | # of hours weekly

(Parish) least valued | 1 | 2 | 3 | 4 | 5 | most valued

(Self) least valued | 1 | 2 | 3 | 4 | 5 | most valued

4. Functioning as a Spiritual Director to members of your parish.

| 1 | 2 | 3 | 4 | 5 | 6 | 7 | 8 | 9 | 10 | + | # of hours weekly

(Parish) least valued | 1 | 2 | 3 | 4 | 5 | most valued

(Self) least valued | 1 | 2 | 3 | 4 | 5 | most valued

5. Exercising disciplilne according to the canons of the Church including counseling as relates to discipline.

| 1 | 2 | 3 | 4 | 5 | 6 | 7 | 8 | 9 | 10 | + | # of hours weekly

(Parish) least valued | 1 | 2 | 3 | 4 | 5 | most valued

(Self) least valued | 1 | 2 | 3 | 4 | 5 | most valued

1. Involved in individual and family pastoral counseling sessions.

| 1 | 2 | 3 | 4 | 5 | 6 | 7 | 8 | 9 | 10 | + | # of hours weekly

(Parish) least valued | 1 | 2 | 3 | 4 | 5 | most valued

(Self) least valued | 1 | 2 | 3 | 4 | 5 | most valued

2. Involved in social activities within the life of the parish itself.

| 1 | 2 | 3 | 4 | 5 | 6 | 7 | 8 | 9 | 10 | + | # of hours weekly

(Parish) least valued | 1 | 2 | 3 | 4 | 5 | most valued

(Self) least valued | 1 | 2 | 3 | 4 | 5 | most valued

3. Involved in social activities within the life of the community outside of the parish.

| 1 | 2 | 3 | 4 | 5 | 6 | 7 | 8 | 9 | 10 | + | # of hours weekly

(Parish) least valued | 1 | 2 | 3 | 4 | 5 | most valued

(Self) least valued | 1 | 2 | 3 | 4 | 5 | most valued

4. Addressing within the public forum social/moral/political issues of the day within the life of the community.

| 1 | 2 | 3 | 4 | 5 | 6 | 7 | 8 | 9 | 10 | + | # of hours weekly

(Parish) least valued | 1 | 2 | 3 | 4 | 5 | most valued

(Self) least valued | 1 | 2 | 3 | 4 | 5 | most valued

5. Serving the administration of your parish's life and that of your primary judicatory outside of your parish.

   ☐1 ☐2 ☐3 ☐4 ☐5 ☐6 ☐7 ☐8 ☐9 ☐10 ☐+   # of hours weekly

   (Parish) least valued ☐1 ☐2 ☐3 ☐4 ☐5   most valued

   (Self) least valued   ☐1 ☐2 ☐3 ☐4 ☐5   most valued

B. BIOGRAPHICAL DATA

	Methodist	Lutheran	Catholic	Anglican
Age	46	48	56	53
Gender	80% M	98% M	100% M	94% M
Ethnicity	96% W	96% W	94% W	100% W
Degrees	32% Adv	38% Adv	58% Adv	22% Adv
Scholar	5%	5%	2%	14%
Priest	5%	5%	82%	62%
Pastor	90%	90%	16%	24%

C. THE WORK WEEK

	Methodist	Lutheran	Catholic	Anglican
Hours	52	48	64	52
Scholarly	37%	40%	30%	41%
Priestly	25%	26%	40%	26%
Pastorally	39%	34%	30%	33%

D. ABBREVIATED CODE FOR QUESTIONNAIRE
(Word = Activity)

Questionnaire
Category-Activity
  Word

SCHOLARLY   1. SERMON
                       2. THEOLOGIANS
                       3. SCRIPTURE
                       4. SPOKESPERSON
                       5. INTELLECTUAL

PRIESTLY   1. WORSHIP
                       2. EUCHARIST
                       3. MINISTRY
                       4. SPIRITUAL DIRECTOR
                       5. DISCIPLINE

PASTORALLY   1. COUNSELING
                       2. PARISH LIFE
                       3. COMMUNITY LIFE
                       4. ISSUES OF THE DAY
                       5. ADMINISTRATION

NB: See Chart E. for Application.

E. COMPARATIVE CHART (% = Affirmative)

S C H O L A R		Methodist PTVA	CTVA	Stress	Lutheran PTVA	CTVA	Stress	Catholic PTVA	CTVA	Stress	Anglican PTVA	CTVA	Stress
	Sermon	72	80		86	88		80	90		74	80	
	Theologians	8	18		12	30		12	34	✓	6	20	✓
	Scripture	20	62	✓	22	56	✓	28	48	✓	28	52	✓
	Spokesperson	48	44		34	32		54	46		24	26	
	Intellectual	24	42	✓	28	34		32	46		36	38	

P R I E S T		Methodist PTVA	CTVA	Stress	Lutheran PTVA	CTVA	Stress	Catholic PTVA	CTVA	Stress	Anglican PTVA	CTVA	Stress
	Worship	90	80		96	92		94	96		90	92	
	Eucharist	38	74		78	94		100	100		96	100	
	Ministry	36	40		64	64		84	84		66	78	
	Sp. Director	42	64		64	66		42	64		24	58	✓
	Discipline	2	28	✓	28	34		9	18		4	6	

E. COMPARATIVE CHART (% = Affirmative) (cont.)

		PTVA	CTVA	Stress	PTVA	CTVA	Stress	PTVA	CTVA	Stress	PTVA	CTVA	Stress
P	Sermon	40	54		50	48		42	40		60	50	
A	Theologians	68	28	✓	48	24	✓	50	38		58	32	✓
S	Scripture	18	22		8	26	✓	12	20		20	28	
T	Spokesperson	10	44	✓	4	26	✓	16	40	✓	20	32	
O	Intellectual	22	40	✓	28	30		30	30		38	34	
R		Methodist			Lutheran			Catholic			Anglican		

PTVA = Parish Task Valuation Assessment

CTVA = Clergy Task Valuation Assessment

ABOUT THE AUTHOR

Dr. John H. Morgan teaches in the summer theology program of the University of Oxford and is John Henry Cardinal Newman Fellow at the Graduate Theological Foundation/USA. Currently Visiting Scholar at Harvard University, he has held postdoctoral appointments at Yale, Princeton, and the University of Notre Dame.